National Standards & Grade-Level Outcomes

for K–12 Physical Education

SHAPE America —
Society of Health and Physical Educators

Principal Writers

Lynn Couturier

Stevie Chepko

Shirley Holt/Hale

SHAPE America

SOCIETY OF HEALTH AND PHYSICAL EDUCATORS

health. moves. minds.

Human Kinetics

Library of Congress Cataloging-in-Publication Data

SHAPE America (Organization)
 National standards & grade-level outcomes for K-12 physical education / by SHAPE America, Society of Health and Physical Educators ; principal writers, Lynn Couturier, Stevie Chepko, Shirley Holt/Hale.
   pages cm
 Includes bibliographical references.
 1. Physical education and training--Study and teaching--United States. 2. Physical fitness--Study and teaching--United States. I. Couturier, Lynn. II. Chepko, Stevie. III. Holt/Hale, Shirley Ann. IV. Title. V. Title: National standards and grade-level outcomes for K-12 physical education.
 GV365.A48 2014
 613.7'071--dc23
                                        2013045506
 ISBN-13: 978-1-4504-9626-1

The web addresses cited in this text were current as of January 2014, unless otherwise noted.

Acquisitions Editors: Scott Wikgren and Ray Vallese; **Principal Editor:** Joe McGavin (SHAPE America); **Developmental Editor:** Ragen E. Sanner; **Assistant Editor:** Elizabeth Evans; **Copyeditor:** Mandy Eastin-Allen; **Permissions Manager:** Dalene Reeder; **Graphic Designer:** Joe Buck; **Graphic Artist:** Denise Lowry; **Cover Designer:** Keith Blomberg; **Photograph (cover):** Left, Fotolia; middle and right, © Human Kinetics; **Photographs (interior):** pp. 1, 3, 5, 7, 9, 15, 16, 39, 40 41, 51, 55, 63, 65, 67, 71, 74, 77, 82, 90, 92, 102, 105, 106, 109 © Human Kinetics; p. 11 dswebb; p. 14 Brand X Pictures; p. 18 Felix Mizioznikov; p. 53 Alina Isakovich; p. 54 laurent hamels; p. 61 Digital Vision; p. 89 Kimberly Reinick; p. 113 Photo courtesy of DigiPrO Photography; **Photo Asset Manager:** Laura Fitch; **Visual Production Assistant:** Joyce Brumfield; **Photo Production Manager:** Jason Allen; **Art Manager:** Kelly Hendren; **Associate Art Manager:** Alan L. Wilborn; **Illustrations:** © Human Kinetics; **Printer:** Premier Print

SHAPE America — Society of Health and Physical Educators (formerly AAHPERD)
1900 Association Drive
Reston, VA 20191
800-213-7193
www.aahperd.org

Printed in the United States of America   10   9   8   7   6   5   4   3

The paper in this book is certified under a sustainable forestry program.

Human Kinetics
Website: www.HumanKinetics.com

United States: Human Kinetics, P.O. Box 5076, Champaign, IL 61825-5076
800-747-4457
e-mail: humank@hkusa.com

Canada: Human Kinetics, 475 Devonshire Road Unit 100, Windsor, ON N8Y 2L5
800-465-7301 (in Canada only)
e-mail: info@hkcanada.com

Europe: Human Kinetics, 107 Bradford Road, Stanningley, Leeds LS28 6AT, United Kingdom
+44 (0) 113 255 5665
e-mail: hk@hkeurope.com

Australia: Human Kinetics, 57A Price Avenue, Lower Mitcham, South Australia 5062
08 8372 0999
e-mail: info@hkaustralia.com

New Zealand: Human Kinetics, P.O. Box 80, Torrens Park, South Australia 5062
0800 222 062
e-mail: info@hknewzealand.com

E6298

Contents

Section II Implementing the Outcomes 63

Preface

Editor's note: Since this book was written, the American Alliance for Health, Physical Education, Recreation and Dance (AAHPERD) changed its name to the Society of Health and Physical Educators, known as SHAPE America. Readers should keep in mind that references hereafter to AAHPERD represent SHAPE America's desire to present an accurate historical context for the book and its development.

In 2011, the board of directors of the National Association for Sport and Physical Education (NASPE)—one of AAHPERD's five national associations—appointed a Curriculum Framework Task Force and charged it with revising the National Standards for K-12 Physical Education as well as with producing a curriculum framework that serves beginning teachers and informs outside constituencies (administrators, parents, policymakers, etc.) about physical education. The task force's primary goal was to provide a bridge between the National Standards, which had last been revised in 2004, and curriculum development by establishing outcomes that delineate what students should know and be able to do at each grade level. A secondary goal was to align the document with the language and goals of the Common Core State Standards (Common Core State Standards Initiative, 2010) in order to position physical education on comparable ground with other school subjects. To accomplish those goals, the task force conducted extensive reviews of current research and best professional practices as well as curriculum frameworks from various states, countries and subject areas.

The task force began its efforts by examining the work of NASPE's Exploratory Curriculum Framework Task Force (2010-2011), which prepared the groundwork and rationale for an AAHPERD curriculum framework. However, neither the exploratory task force nor the Curriculum Framework Task Force had to start from scratch. The foundation for the standards and outcomes in this document were laid by three earlier professional works: the first and second editions of *Moving Into the Future: National Standards for Physical Education* (NASPE, 1995, 2004) and *Outcomes of Quality Physical Education Programs* (NASPE, 1992).

Throughout this project, the task force focused on several key points:

- Ensuring that the standards and outcomes are measurable and that their wording reflects the content that we teach.
- Integrating language that parallels the Common Core State Standards where possible.
- Using research and member feedback to guide development of the document.
- Producing resources in formats that serve practitioners effectively.

Like all SHAPE America documents, this one has been subjected to several member reviews (May 2012, November 2012 and February 2013) as well as targeted reviews by groups with specific expertise (Society of State Leaders of Health and Physical Education, November 2012; middle and secondary school teachers of the year, January 2013; and the NASPE Board of Directors, March 2013). To ensure a broad reach, the document was sent directly to the leadership of the state AAHPERD associations. It also was shared at conferences, including the Physical Education Institute (July 2012), NASPE's Physical Education Teacher Education Conference (October 2012) and the AAHPERD National Convention & Expo (April 2013). All member feedback was considered carefully throughout the process, and it shaped and enhanced the final product.

About SHAPE America and AAHPERD

Effective December 2013, AAHPERD changed its name to the Society of Health and Physical Educations, known as SHAPE America. The organization is poised to move forward in creating a new chapter in its 128-year history with a new name, vision and mission. A new logo, tagline and brand for the organization, as well as a new website, are to be introduced in 2014.

SHAPE America is the organization's seventh name change since its founding in 1885 as the Association for the Advancement of Physical Education. Earlier in 2013, the organization voted unanimously to unify what had been five national associations—including the National Association for Sport and Physical Education (NASPE)—under the AAHPERD umbrella.

To maintain historical accuracy in this book, both AAHPERD and NASPE are cited as generators of the current National Standards & Grade-Level Outcomes for K-12 Physical Education, because the effort to revise the National Standards began with a task force appointed by the NASPE board of directors and culminated with the acceptance of the new standards by the AAHPERD board of directors.

The largest organization of physical educators in the country, with close to 20,000 members, SHAPE America published the first-ever set of National Standards for Physical Education in 1995, developed the Let's Move in School public-awareness campaign to increase physical activity before, during and after school, and originated the Shape of the Nation Report, which reviews the status of physical education across the United States, among its many professional firsts.

Through its new name, SHAPE America will work to:

- Shape a future in which healthy is the norm.
- Shape a standard of excellence in health education and physical education.
- Shape the lifelong habits of young people.
- Shape and influence policy related to physical education and school health education.

Among its many partners, SHAPE America works with the Alliance for a Healthier Generation, American Heart Association, The Cooper Institute, First Lady Michelle Obama's Let's Move! initiative and the President's Council on Fitness, Sports & Nutrition.

Acknowledgments

SHAPE America—formerly the American Alliance for Health, Physical Education, Recreation and Dance (AAHPERD)—is indebted to the members of the AAHPERD Curriculum Framework Task Force for leading the process of revising the National Standards for K-12 Physical Education and developing the Grade-Level Outcomes for K-12 Physical Education. SHAPE America also appreciates the many professionals who reviewed drafts of the standards and outcomes and made valuable contributions that strengthened the document. Among these professionals, several deserve special recognition for the thoroughness of their work, including Nancy Schmitz, John Kruse, Tina Hall, Chuck Corbin, and Missy Parker and her graduate students at Northern Colorado University.

AAHPERD Curriculum Framework Task Force

Lynn Couturier, task force chair, SUNY Cortland

Stevie Chepko, Washington, D.C.

Shirley Holt/Hale, Oak Ridge, TN

Dan Persse, Blaine, WA

Brad Rettig, Lincoln, NE

Georgi Roberts, Fort Worth, TX

SHAPE America also appreciates and acknowledges the exceptional foundation for this document built by previous task forces and committees, with the support of the board of directors of the National Association for Sport and Physical Education, formerly one of the five associations comprising AAHPERD. These groups include the 1995 Standards and Assessment Task Force, the Second Edition Writing Committee and the 2010 Exploratory Curriculum Framework Task Force.

2010 Exploratory Curriculum Framework Task Force

Derrick Mears, chair, Western Washington University

Meggin DeMoss, Rose Hill, KS

Shaunna McGhie, Utah Valley University

Peter Rattigan, Rowan University

Suggested citation for this book:

Society of Health and Physical Educators. (2014). *National standards & grade-level outcomes for K-12 physical education.* Champaign, IL: Human Kinetics.

SHAPE America — Society of Health and Physical Educators (formerly AAHPERD)
E. Paul Roetert, CEO
Cheryl Richardson, Senior Director of Member Engagement & Programming

Section I

Exploring the National Standards & Grade-Level Outcomes

Chapter 1

Developing a Curriculum Framework

This book is designed to be a tool for preservice teachers and practitioners to use in planning curricula; designing units, lessons and practice tasks; and assessing and tracking student progress across grades. In addition, it provides others invested in the education process (e.g., administrators, boards of education, parents, policymakers) with a framework for understanding what students should know and be able to do as a result of instruction in physical education. To aid readers' understanding of the concepts and tools used throughout the book, terms appearing in **blue** have been included with definitions in the glossary in the back of the book.

It's clear that many people have misconceptions about physical education and, consequently, might question its value in schools. This resource provides external constituencies with the information they need to understand contemporary physical education and hold programs accountable for student learning.

The revision of the National Standards for K-12 Physical Education and development of the Grade-Level Outcomes for K-12 Physical Education was influenced by a variety of other curriculum frameworks, the Common Core State Standards, and current disciplinary knowledge and research in physical education. With the Common Core in mind, these physical education **content standards** and outcomes are written to reflect the content (knowledge and skills) that we expect students to learn in physical education (Common Core State Standards Initiative, 2010a; Penney & Chandler, 2000). Throughout this document, the focus is on student learning, in concurrence with Ennis (2011) that physical education "that promotes motor skill competence and knowledge growth . . . contributes to the educational mission of schools" (p. 16). This is in contrast to the notion of physical education as recreation, or simply physical activity, which is not centered on student learning and not aligned with the goals of public education.

In addition, these standards and outcomes are written in a manner that is measurable in order to facilitate the assessment and tracking of student progress. The Grade-Level Outcomes provide a progressive scope and sequence that leads to the achievement of the standards and, ultimately, to a physically literate individual who is ready for college or a career and a physically active life (Common Core State Standards Initiative, 2010a). This chapter summarizes the changes that have been made to the standards since the second edition of *Moving Into the Future: National Standards for Physical Education* (NASPE, 2004) as well as the research that guided the Curriculum Framework Task Force in its revisions of the standards and the development of Grade-Level Outcomes for K-12 Physical Education.

Key Changes to the Standards

This is the third iteration of the K-12 physical education standards. The first change that most readers will notice is the incorporation of the term *physical literacy* in the goal of physical education. As used in this book, physical literacy is "the ability to move with competence and confidence in a wide variety of physical activities in multiple environments that benefit the healthy development of the whole person" (Mandigo, Francis, Lodewyk & Lopez, 2012, p. 28; Whitehead, 2001). It supports the holistic development of students by encompassing all three domains of physical education (**psychomotor**, **cognitive** and **affective**). It includes not only physical competence and knowledge but also the

attitudes, motivation and social and psychological skills needed for participation (Penney & Chandler, 2000, pp. 80-81). The term *physical literacy* is comprehensive in conveying what we are trying to accomplish in physical education. It also parallels terminology used currently in other subject areas, such as *health literacy* and *math literacy*. Its inclusion in the goal of physical education puts physical education in step with other school subjects and the intent of the Common Core State Standards (Common Core State Standards Initiative, 2010b).

The second substantial change is the combining of Standards 3 and 4 into one standard, now Standard 3, making for five National Standards instead of six. The reduction in the number of standards is not unprecedented. The second edition of *Moving Into the Future* reduced the number of standards from seven to six. Standards 3 and 4 (2004) were written in a way that conveys the goal of physical education rather than the content we teach, or "content standard" language as can be seen below:

Standard 3 (2004): A physically educated person participates regularly in physical activity.

Standard 4 (2004): A physically educated person achieves and maintains a health-enhancing level of physical fitness.

This edition of the National Standards for K-12 Physical Education seeks to retain the key concepts of the two standards while using language that reflects the content we teach in physical education class. Given the constraints of physical education classes in schools, it is difficult for physical education teachers to ensure that students participate regularly in physical activity or achieve physical fitness. We do, however, give our students the knowledge and skills needed for achieving and maintaining health-related fitness and participating in lifelong physical activity. The knowledge and skills we teach form the basis of the revised content standard:

Standard 3 (2013): The physically literate individual demonstrates the knowledge and skills to achieve and maintain a health-enhancing level of physical activity and fitness.

The other standards have some minor editorial revisions but are very similar to those in the second edition (NASPE, 2004).

What truly sets this edition of the National Standards for K-12 Physical Education apart is the inclusion of grade-level outcomes. Practitioners long have identified grade-level outcomes as a missing component in designing and implementing a standards-based curriculum, particularly after *Outcomes of Quality Physical Education Programs* (NASPE, 1992) went out of publication. The grade-level outcomes in this book are organized by level (elementary, middle and high school) as well as by standard. The scope and sequence of the outcomes extends from kindergarten through high school to facilitate curriculum design across all levels, not just within one level. All outcomes are written to align with the standards and with the intent of fostering lifelong physical activity.

Research in motor development provided the foundation for the development of grade-level outcomes. While Clark and Metcalfe (1997) might use a mountain metaphor and Gallahue, Ozmun and Goodway (2012) a triangulated hourglass, all agree that motor development is a dynamic process that is affected by the interaction of the individual, the movement tasks and the environmental context. Key factors in the process of motor development are opportunities for practice, encouragement, instruction and environmental context (Gallahue et al., 2012, p. 52). The decision about when to provide practice, encouragement and instruction is based on identified stages of motor development, just as these stages form the framework for the grade-level outcomes.

Gallahue et al. (2012) identify the fundamental motor phase as occurring between ages 5 and 7. At this stage, learners explore and experiment with a range of movements in a variety of environmental contexts. The goal in this period, according to Clark and Metcalfe (1997), is the development of a motor repertoire that later will allow for more skilled actions tailored to specific movement contexts (p. 15). This emerging phase is followed by a more context-specific period (Clark & Metcalfe, 1997) or a specialized movement phase (Gallahue et al., 2012) in upper elementary grades, where skills are **maturing**. Learners in upper elementary school begin to combine and apply **fundamental motor skills** in more specialized movement contexts. The fundamental motor skills are then refined and executed with more control and **accuracy**, leading to **mature patterns**.

Beginning in middle school, most learners enter the application stage (Gallahue et al., 2012), in which increases in cognitive development allow learners to refine and use skills in **modified game** play or to participate in more complex fitness activities. Learners understand and apply rules and context-specific knowledge based on environmental constraints imposed within games or fitness activities. It is at this point that learners begin to make choices about the types of activities that interest them or provide them with chances for enjoyment. The development of motor skills becomes increasingly more individualized (Clark & Metcalfe, 1997, p. 18) during middle school and continues through high school in the lifelong utilization stage (Gallahue et al., 2012). This is the culmination of the previous stages, and learners will begin to refine and improve movement competencies based on interest, opportunities for participation, motivation and talent. Outcomes for the middle and high school levels reflect these developmental stages. While middle school provides learners with opportunities in a wide variety of activities, high school affords learners choices based on personal interest.

Guiding Research

In reviewing the current literature in physical education, the task force identified several areas as critical to the direction and development of grade-level outcomes: motor skill competency, student engagement and intrinsic motivation, instructional climate, gender differences, lifetime activity approach and physical activity. Brief summaries of the findings are presented for each of these areas, followed by a synopsis of how the findings were applied in the grade-level outcomes.

Motor Skill Competency

A growing body of evidence indicates that motor skill **competency** is essential for participation in physical activity and for health-enhancing fitness. Spessato, Gabbard and Valentini (2013) found that during physical education class, motor skill competence of children ages 5 to 10 proved to be a better predictor of physical activity levels than body mass index. In their study of the relationship between motor skill proficiency and physical activity, Stodden et al. (2008) concluded that "motor skill competence is a critically important, yet underestimated, causal mechanism for the health-risk behavior of physical inactivity" (p. 302). Lack of motor skill proficiency was associated with lower physical activity levels and, consequently, lower fitness levels. Other researchers have corroborated these findings, with many noting the importance of emphasizing skill development in physical education as a strategy to promote physical activity participation and fitness (Barnett, van Beurden, Morgan, Brooks & Beard, 2008a,b; Castelli & Valley, 2007; Hamilton & White, 2008; Kambas et al., 2012; Stodden et al., 2008; Stodden, Langendorfer & Roberton, 2009; Strong et al., 2005). It should be noted that physical education is uniquely positioned within schools to foster motor skill competence.

Student Engagement and Intrinsic Motivation

Students in physical education do not acquire the knowledge and skills needed to be physically active if they are not personally engaged in the content. Some students feel alienated in physical education and opt out completely (Carlson, 1995; Ntoumanis, Pensgaard, Martin & Pipe, 2004; Shen, Wingert, Weidong, Haichun & Rukavina, 2010). While these students might constitute only a small percentage of the student body in a school, other students might be participating passively by taking their places in the activity but not making an effort to engage fully. This behavior might mask their disengagement, but it clearly does not enhance student learning. It's essential for teachers to create a learning environment that fosters engagement for all students in their classes.

Research on intrinsic motivation in physical education, particularly through the framework of self-determination theory, has yielded a great deal of information about which factors influence student engagement. These factors include perceived competence, autonomy (choice of activity), relatedness, cognitive demand and social comparison. Students' perceived competence and self-efficacy have been found to positively predict physical activity levels (Bevans, Fitzpatrick, Sanchez & Forest, 2010; Gao, Lee, Solmon & Zhang, 2009; Hamilton & White, 2008; Stuart, Biddle, O'Donovan & Nevill, 2005). Perceived competence also is associated with higher levels of enjoyment of physical activity (Gao, Lee & Harrison, 2012; Smith & St. Pierre, 2009). Students who don't believe they are competent in a particular activity are less likely to be interested in participating during physical education class or outside of class (Garn, Cothran & Jenkins, 2011; Ntoumanis et al., 2004; Portman, 2003; Shen et al., 2010). Clearly, if students are to be physically active throughout their lives, they need to learn skills well enough to feel competent during participation.

In addition, choice of activity is important for student engagement and motivation. When students have the opportunity to choose their activity or a variation of the learning task, it contributes to feelings of autonomy and leads to

higher motivation levels (Bryan, Sims, Hester & Dunaway, 2013; Hannon & Ratcliffe, 2005; Ntoumanis et al., 2004; Prusak, Treasure, Darst & Pangrazi, 2004; Ward, Wilkinson, Graser & Prusak, 2008; Zhang, Solmon, Kosma, Carlson & Gu, 2011).

Relatedness is another element that contributes to motivation and engagement. Students who experience higher levels of relatedness through social support and encouragement by teachers and peers are more likely to be engaged than those who do not (Dunton et al., 2012; Gao, Lee, Ping & Kosam, 2011; Haerens, Kirk, Cardon, De Bourdeauhuij & Vansteenkiste, 2010; Ntoumanis et al., 2004; Zhang et al., 2011). Ensuring that learning tasks have challenging cognitive demands can also increase student engagement and situational interest (Chen & Darst, 2001; Smith & St. Pierre, 2009; Subramaniam, 2009). However, engagement and motivation can be diminished when students—particularly adolescents—are placed in situations in which social evaluation or comparisons are readily made by peers (Garn, Ware & Solmon, 2011; Ntoumanis et al., 2004; Ommundsen, 2006). Often, this is the case in competitive activities that require high levels of skill.

Instructional Climate

Much has been written about the instructional climate in physical education. Bevans et al. (2010) found that student engagement was enhanced by a mastery climate and that skill development within a lesson can increase engagement among students with lower perceived competence. Many other researchers have echoed the importance of a mastery climate, which is task-centered and focuses on self-improvement, for student engagement and development of motor skill competence (Ennis, 2011; Gao et al., 2011; Hamilton & White, 2008; Ntoumanis et al., 2004; Ommundsen, 2006; Standage, Duda & Ntoumanis, 2003; Treasure & Roberts, 2001).

Another aspect of the instructional climate is the degree to which competition (performance) is emphasized. High levels of traditional game play, which contribute to a competitive environment, have been found to alienate less-skilled students (Bevans et al., 2010; Ntoumanis et al., 2004). Garn, Cothran, et al. (2011) noted that "large-sided team games with minimal learning progressions or skill development during the semester forced students to build competence in a structure that catered to students who were already highly skilled" (p. 233). Girls, less-skilled students and overweight students preferred more cooperative activities or noncompetitive activities over competitive ones, indicating that highly skilled students took the games too seriously, dominated play and sometimes excluded them from participation (Bernstein, Phillips & Silverman, 2011; Bevans et al., 2010; Portman, 2003). Competitive games appeal mainly to highly skilled boys and girls who experience positive reinforcement in that setting while less-skilled students were more likely to experience negative social evaluation and embarrassment (Garn, Cothran, et al., 2011; Hill & Hannon, 2008).

Gender Differences

Many researchers have examined the role of gender in the physical education setting and have found that as children mature, differences become more pronounced. In general, girls are less physically active than boys, and as they age, that trend continues or worsens (Bradley, McMurray, Harrell & Deng, 2000;

Haerens et al., 2010; Hannon & Ratcliffe, 2005; Pangrazi, Corbin & Welk, 1996; Patnode et al., 2011; Prochaska, Sallis, Slymen & McKenzie, 2003; Treanor, Graber, Housner & Weigand, 1998; Xiang, McBride & Guan, 2004; Yli-Piipari, Leskinen, Jaakola & Liukkonen, 2012). Researchers also have explored the activity preferences of boys and girls and found some divergence, particularly during adolescence. Girls tend to prefer noncompetitive and cooperative activities, dance, fitness and activities that provide opportunities for social interaction (Azzarito & Solmon, 2009; Bevans et al., 2010; Couturier, Chepko & Coughlin, 2007; Grieser et al., 2006; Hill & Hannon, 2008; O'Neill, Pate & Liese, 2011; Prusak et al., 2004; Ruiz, Graupera, Morena & Rico, 2010; Wilkinson & Bretzing, 2011; Xu & Liu, 2013). Similarly, Eime et al. (2013) found that fewer than 50 percent of the adolescent girls they studied met the physical activity guidelines and, as they aged, their preferences shifted from competitive and organized activities to noncompetitive, nonorganized activities. Gao et al. (2012) found that girls perceived themselves as having lower ability in traditional team sports and activities stereotyped as masculine. With the exception of the highly skilled, most girls are dissatisfied with the traditional team sports curriculum (Bryan et al., 2013; Derry, 2002; Hannon & Ratcliffe, 2005; Hill & Hannon, 2008).

Researchers also have examined the effect of the environment on student engagement and found that girls are more likely than boys to report factors such as showering, changing, and messing up their appearance as barriers to participation (Couturier et al., 2007; Grieser et al., 2006; Xu & Liu, 2013). Perhaps girls' lower physical activity levels are understandable when considering that the traditional curriculum and typical physical education setting do not meet their needs or interests (Couturier et al., 2007; Trost et al., 1997).

Lifetime Activities Approach

Finally, there is strong support for a health-enhancing and lifetime physical activity approach in physical education. As long as two decades ago, Corbin et al. (1994) argued that the Lifetime Activity Model, focused on lifetime activities with enough energy expenditure to attain health benefits, was more appropriate for children and adolescents than the Exercise Prescription Model adopted by adults and athletes. Since that time, many researchers have argued that physical education should focus on health-promoting physical activity practices and a curriculum that teaches lifelong activities (Balestracci, 2013; Castelli & Valley, 2007; Corbin, 2002; Grieser et al., 2006; Pangrazi, 2010; Penney & Chandler, 2000; Sallis et al., 2012; Wang, Castelli, Liu, Bian & Tan, 2010). When students learn skills that they can use across the life span, that have personal or cultural meaning and that can be performed alone or with a partner (instead of a group or team), it's more likely that they will continue physical activity through adulthood (Pangrazi et al., 1996).

Research on the importance of physical activity for good health also influenced the development of the National Standards & Grade-Level Outcomes for K-12 Physical Education (Bryan et al, 2013; Corbin, Pangrazi & Le Masurier, 2004; U.S. Department of Health and Human Services, 2008). *Physical Activity Guidelines for Americans* recommends that children ages 6 to 17 should participate in at least 60 minutes of physical activity daily. Because children spend a large portion of their day in school, the Institute of Medicine further recommends that at least 30 minutes—or half of the daily recommended time—be accumulated during the school day (Institute of Medicine of the National Academies, 2013). For some children—particularly minorities and children from lower socioeconomic backgrounds—physical education might be the only opportunity they have for physical activity (Basch, 2010; Prochaska et al., 2003).

Numerous studies have documented diminishing physical activity levels as children move into adolescence (Bradley et al., 2000; Corbin et al., 2004; Patnode et al., 2011; Prochaska et al., 2003; Xu & Liu, 2013; Yli-Piipari et al., 2012). While physical education cannot be the sole solution to the problems of increasingly sedentary lifestyles and childhood obesity, it is in an excellent position to influence physical activity levels during the school day and beyond (Institute of Medicine of the National Academies, 2013; Sallis et al., 2012). In addition to having children and adolescents participate in at least 60 minutes of physical activity daily, it's important that most of that time be spent in moderate to vigorous physical activity (MVPA) and, on at least three days a week, students should participate in muscle- and bone-strengthening activities (U.S. Department of Health and Human Services, 2008). SHAPE America guidelines further recommend that students engage in MVPA for at least 50 percent of physical education class time (NASPE, 2009a,b,c).

Quality physical education is the foundation for student attainment of the physical activity guidelines, providing students with opportunities for physical activity and the development of skills and knowledge during school. Students can then use these same skills and knowledge in before- and after-school physical activity programs, recess and classroom physical activity breaks (NASPE, 2008). It is the responsibility of physical education teachers to take on a leadership role in creating physically active schools and communities. They are uniquely qualified to sponsor and support new physical activity programs and classroom activities, guide classroom teachers in their efforts to include nutrition and fitness in their subject areas, and advocate for student and community access to facilities and equipment.

To help practitioners meet the physical activity guidelines, several researchers have focused on how to increase MVPA time in physical education classes (Lounsbery, McKenzie, Trost & Smith, 2011; McKenzie et al., 2004; McKenzie, Prochaska, Sallis & LaMaster, 2004; Sallis et al., 2012; Schuldheisz & van der Mars, 2001; Van Buerden et al., 2003). In most cases, MVPA decreases during skill acquisition, but given the importance of skill competency for lifelong physical activity and fitness, practitioners need to find ways to optimize MVPA during instructional time.

Strategies such as keeping groups small, allowing for choice in activity or variation of learning tasks, designing tasks with appropriate levels of challenge; and practicing in **dynamic environments** and **small-sided games** foster a mastery climate while keeping physical activity levels high. These practices are reinforced throughout the grade-level outcomes that follow and in chapter 7 (specifically, the section on creating a mastery climate).

Application of Findings

SHAPE America considers the development of motor skill competence to be the highest priority in the grade-level outcomes. As research has shown, skill competency is essential for student engagement, intrinsic motivation, perceived competency, participation in physical activity and, subsequently, sufficient levels of health-related fitness. It is the key to attaining the goal of physical education: a physically literate individual. The grade-level outcomes in this book address the need to develop skillfulness in part by focusing on the acquisition of fundamental motor skills at the elementary level. These are the building blocks for all specialized movement patterns that students will use in adolescence and adulthood to participate in a variety of fitness and physical activities as well as organized sport.

Skill competency is formed through sufficient, **deliberate practice** (Ericsson, 2006). That requires carefully planned progressions, meaningful and well-designed learning tasks, unit lengths that allow for skill acquisition, and

specific, corrective feedback. All of those factors are critical components of an instructional climate that focuses on mastery. A mastery climate promotes the development of skill competency while enabling less-skilled students to be successful in physical education classes. It also can enhance perceived competence and student engagement while limiting the opportunities for social comparison associated with a performance or competitive climate. In this instructional environment, students are focused on self-improvement and practice skills in dynamic environments and small-sided games, which facilitate maximal practice opportunities and skill acquisition. These types of learning activities also have the advantage of keeping MVPA levels high.

The grade-level outcomes in this book were designed to facilitate skill development and the implementation of a mastery climate by using comprehensive, developmentally appropriate progressions across grade levels for the skills and knowledge associated with each national standard. These progressions are readily seen in the outcomes and in the Scope & Sequence for K-12 Physical Education chart (see table 6.1 in chapter 6). At the same time, SHAPE America recognizes that good progressions are not enough to ensure learning. Practitioners must be able to design appropriate learning tasks as well as monitor and track student progress. For those reasons, the standards and outcomes are supplemented with chapters on designing practice tasks and assessing student learning. In addition, the introductions to the chapters on the middle and high school levels include recommendations about the length of units to help practitioners allot an appropriate amount of instructional time for the activities.

SHAPE America also considers the traditional (and gendered) team sport curriculum to be a concern for the profession. The evidence clearly indicates that this type of competitive sport curriculum alienates many students, particularly girls and less-skilled students. It does little to address the need for skills and knowledge that promote lifetime physical activity or health-related fitness. In general, the grade-level outcomes that follow eliminate full-sided games and de-emphasize competitive activities.

SHAPE America does recognize that competitive team sports (invasion games) have attributes such as cultural relevance and opportunities for affiliation that merit inclusion in the curriculum. However, their inclusion is limited to the middle school level and only in small-sided games formats that maximize practice and physical activity opportunities for students. By the time students reach the high school level, invasion games no longer are part of the curriculum as the focus shifts to lifetime activities and health-related fitness.

The grade-level outcomes are structured so that activity categories that appeal to less-skilled students and many girls are integrated throughout the middle and high school levels. These categories include fitness activities, outdoor pursuits and dance, which are noncompetitive and are lifelong physical activities. In addition, activity choices within these categories should vary each year across the middle and high school levels to support student engagement (Mears, 2008). The practice of teaching the same activities and sports each year in the traditional curriculum cannot be supported in an educational environment.

The grade-level outcomes provide a scope and sequence of skills and knowledge predicated on teaching a variety of activities to achieve learning for all students. Finally, the importance of lifetime activities and health-related fitness can be seen at all levels in the outcomes but become the central focus of the high school level, particularly in Standard 3. Students should graduate from high school well-prepared to participate in selected lifelong physical activities and knowledgeable about achieving and maintaining their own health-related fitness.

Many factors that affect the quality of physical education—including class length, class size, time allotment within the school day and program budgets—generally are beyond the control of the teacher. However, it is noteworthy that most of the components described in the research for the grade-level outcomes are well within the physical education teacher's domain. The teacher can have a tremendous impact on the development of skill competency, the establishment of a mastery climate and the engagement of all students, regardless of ability. It is SHAPE America's intention that this document becomes an essential resource for physical educators, both new and experienced, in creating and enhancing high-quality programs that promote student learning.

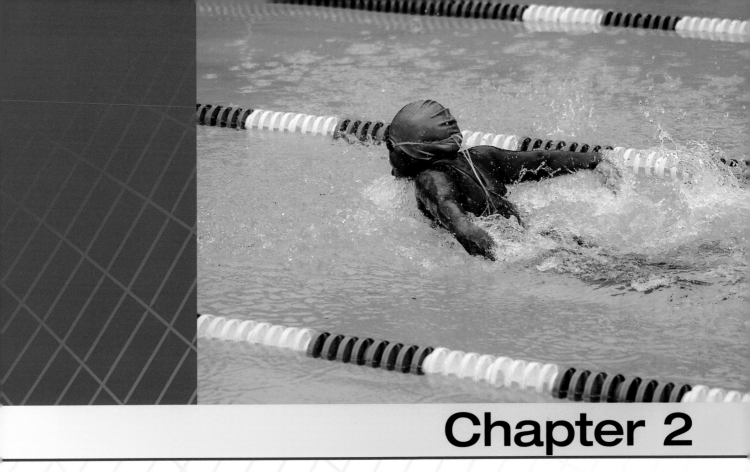

National Standards for K-12 Physical Education

The goal of physical education is to develop physically literate individuals who have the knowledge, skills and confidence to enjoy a lifetime of healthful physical activity.

To pursue a lifetime of healthful physical activity, a physically literate individual

- Has learned the skills necessary to participate in a variety of physical activities.
- Knows the implications and the benefits of involvement in various types of physical activities.
- Participates regularly in physical activity.
- Is physically fit.
- Values physical activity and its contributions to a healthful lifestyle.

This definition of a physically literate individual was adapted from the work of Mandigo, Francis, Lodewyk, and Lopez (2012) and the definition of a physically educated person in NASPE (2004).

The National Standards for K-12 Physical Education and the accompanying grade-level outcomes give physical educators a framework for producing physically literate individuals, setting students on the road to enjoying a lifetime of healthful physical activity.

National Standards for K-12 Physical Education

Standard 1
The physically literate individual demonstrates competency in a variety of motor skills and movement patterns.

Standard 2
The physically literate individual applies knowledge of concepts, principles, strategies and tactics related to movement and performance.

Standard 3
The physically literate individual demonstrates the knowledge and skills to achieve and maintain a health-enhancing level of physical activity and fitness.

Standard 4
The physically literate individual exhibits responsible personal and social behavior that respects self and others.

Standard 5
The physically literate individual recognizes the value of physical activity for health, enjoyment, challenge, self-expression and/or social interaction.

Note: The standards are not prioritized in a particular order.

Figure 2.1 represents the process of achieving the National Standards through physical education, helping learners attain the goal of living a physically active lifestyle. This roadmap illustrates the emphasis of the outcomes at each level and conveys the idea that there are many ways to accomplish this.

Reading the Grade-Level Outcomes

The grade-level outcomes have several organizing features to help readers locate the information they want. First, the outcomes are grouped by elementary, middle and high school levels. Second, each outcome has been assigned a number, although the numbers do not reflect any particular priority. The number of the outcome is also affiliated with

- A standard (S1, S2, S3, S4 or S5).
- A school level [elementary (E), middle (M) or high (H) school].
- A grade level [K, 1, 2, 3, 4, 5, 6, 7, 8 or high school level 1 (L1) or level 2 (L2)].

For example:

- S2.E1.3 refers to Standard 2, Elementary Outcome 1, Grade 3.
- S1.M12.7 refers to Standard 1, Middle School Outcome 12, Grade 7.
- S5.H3.L1 refers to Standard 5, High School Outcome 3, Level 1.

The coding system should make it easier to locate particular outcomes. Finally, at the middle and high school levels, activities have been grouped by type or category, with which the reader will need to be familiar while reviewing the outcomes.

- **Outdoor pursuits:** The outdoor environment is an important factor in student engagement in the activity. Outdoor pursuits might include but are not limited to recreational boating (e.g., kayaking, canoeing, sailing, rowing); hiking; backpacking; fishing; orienteering or geocaching; ice skating; skateboarding; snow or water skiing; snowboarding; snowshoeing; surfing; bouldering,

The Road to a Lifetime of Physical Activity

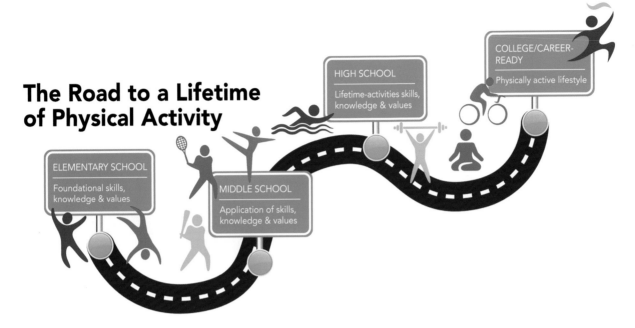

Figure 2.1 The road to a lifetime of physical activity is a long one, full of learning, experiences and the happiness and satisfaction that comes with physical literacy.

traversing/climbing; mountain biking; adventure activities; and ropes courses. The selection of activities depends on the environmental opportunities within the geographical region.

- **Fitness activities:** Activities with a focus on improving or maintaining fitness. Fitness activities might include but are not limited to yoga, Pilates, resistance training, spinning, running, fitness walking, fitness swimming, kickboxing, cardio–kick, Zumba and exergaming.

- **Dance and rhythmic activities:** Activities that focus on dance or rhythms. Dance and rhythmic activities might include but are not limited to dance forms such as creative movement or dance, ballet, modern, ethnic or folk, hip hop, Latin, line, ballroom, social and square.

- **Aquatics:** Might include but are not limited to swimming, diving, synchronized swimming and water polo.

- **Individual-performance activities:** Might include but are not limited to gymnastics, figure skating, track and field, multisport events, inline skating, wrestling, self-defense and skateboarding.

- **Games and sports:** Includes the following games categories: **invasion, net/wall, target** and **fielding/striking**.

- **Lifetime activities:** Includes the categories of outdoor pursuits, selected individual-performance activities, aquatics and net/wall and target games. Invasion and fielding/striking games are not included in the high school outcomes because they require team participation and are less suited to lifelong participation.

Chapter 3

Elementary School-Level Outcomes (K-Grade 5)

The elementary school years long have been recognized as critical in the development of **fundamental motor skills**. From the early work of Wickstrom (1970) and Espenschade and Eckert (1967) to that of Clark and Metcalfe (2002) and Gallahue et al. (2012), the years of upper childhood (ages 6 through 10) are considered to be the years of "perfection and stabilization" of the skills first appearing in early childhood (Rarick, 1961). Gallahue et al. (2012) refer to the elementary school years as the **emerging** stage for fundamental motor skills with a reminder that these skills are not determined maturationally; rather, they are determined by "opportunities for practice, encouragement and instruction . . . with conditions of the learning environment playing important roles in the degree to which the fundamental movement skills develop" (pp. 52-53). Teachers of elementary physical education control these factors and are key players in the development of fundamental motor skills.

Because elementary school is the foundation for the development of fundamental motor skills, it is imperative that the focus of physical education be on skill acquisition. The days of "busy, happy and good" activities (Placek, 1983) in elementary school physical education are gone. Emerging skills become mature skills only with deliberate practice and quality instruction. The fundamental motor skills of elementary school form the building blocks for game play, physical activity and fitness activities that follow in middle and high school. Children who leave elementary school without a strong foundation of motor skills are "left behind" in the same manner as children without the prerequisite skills in language and mathematics (Clark, 2007). Skill acquisition, then, is essential for continued participation in physical activity in adolescence and beyond (Barnett et al., 2010; Gallahue et al., 2011; Stodden et al., 2009).

Just as elementary physical education is the environment for the development and mastery of fundamental motor skills, it is in elementary school physical education that children experience the joys and frustrations of becoming competent movers. Research supports success and enjoyment in those early years of physical education as critical to future involvement in physical activity (Bengoechea, Sabiston, Ahmed, & Farnoush, 2010; Corbin, 2001; Ennis, 2010). However, enjoyment and success do not preclude the focused practice necessary for skill acquisition. When tasks are developmentally appropriate for children in a learning environment that is noncompetitive with a focus on personal growth, skill practice is enjoyable. Skill practice, designed developmentally, leads to success; success leads to continued practice and mature patterns.

Guidance for Using Elementary School Outcomes

The National Standards and the grade-level outcomes for elementary school physical education are based on the tenets of skill acquisition, enjoyment and success. The outcomes are designed to foster the maturing of the fundamental motor skills and the developing understanding of **movement concepts** and fitness principles. Success is measured in terms of self-mastery (i.e., achieving the outcomes or improving movement competency).

The focus of the elementary outcomes is on mature patterns, not on traditional games, the stunts of Olympic gymnastics or calisthenics in large groups. In fact, games don't even *appear* in the elementary-level outcomes. The outcomes are a developmentally appropriate progression from introduction to maturity of the skill.

Outcomes are based on motor development research, children's developmental levels and past experiences in physical education.

Adjustments in grade-level outcomes might be needed based on children's past experiences or number of days per week of instructional physical education. Children who have instructional physical education only one or two days per week will not reach mature pattern execution as quickly as those with more frequent instructional physical education and guided practice. While that can be very frustrating for the elementary physical education teacher, it must not serve as an excuse for anything less than high-quality programs. *Note:* Find guidance in developing high-quality programs in AAHPERD's *Appropriate Instructional Practice Guidelines* (2009) and *Opportunity to Learn Guidelines* (2010). Those documents will assist greatly in decisions regarding best practices that reflect the National Standards.

Elementary school physical education should provide breadth in experiences relative to each emerging skill. Breadth, however, does not equate to mere exposure. Lessons in elementary school physical education and selected

Skill Practice and Revisitation

Example: An elementary school physical educator teaches a series of lessons with a skill focus (e.g., the overhand throw). At the end of the theme or unit, the assessment is made indicating a mature pattern of skill execution. Feeling a bit of accomplishment, the teacher moves the students forward to the next skill with very little if any revisitation of the overhand throw. The class progresses to the middle school only to hear the physical education teacher exclaim, "If only they had learned to throw correctly in elementary school!"

tasks and learning experiences should move the learner toward skill maturity. A single lesson focused on a skill will not produce a mature pattern. A one-time demonstration of a mature pattern will not guarantee continued mature execution of the skill or performance of the skill in a variety of contexts. Deliberate practice and revisitation of the skill are necessary to achieve and maintain a mature pattern of the skill (see chapter 6).

Yes, teaching for skill acquisition and assessment is critical for student learning; however, revisitation and a variety of practice environments are essential components of high-quality teaching for skill development and retention of student learning.

Outcomes for Standards 1 and 2 in elementary school physical education are centered around skill development in the areas of games skills, educational gymnastics and dance. The outcomes focus on the skills within the areas of **locomotors**, **nonlocomotors or stability** and **manipulatives**. Standard 1 outcomes focus on *emerging* skills for elementary students. They are emerging fundamental motor skills, with "increases in motor efficiency" and "increasingly consistent motor patterns" leading to skilled motor performance in a variety of contexts (Haywood, 1986, p. 99). Motor efficiency and consistent **motor patterns** do not happen by chance, nor do they appear simply through participation in physical activity. Emerging motor skills become maturing motor skills through emphasis on **critical elements**, guided and deliberate practice and targeted feedback.

The basic locomotor and manipulative skills in Standard 1 are accompanied by suggested critical elements that provide an analysis of each skill by its components. Pages 18-25 list critical elements for each of the locomotor and manipulative skills in Standard 1. Grade-level outcomes provide a progression of mastery of critical elements leading to the maturing pattern of the skill; mastery of the components across grade levels leads to mature patterns in grades 4 and 5. Children in the emerging stage of skill development benefit from the introduction of a single performance element (e.g., opposite foot forward), practice and mastery of that performance component before being introduced to the next critical element of the skill. **Differentiated instruction** provides the appropriate critical element for each child's developmental and emerging skill level.

The cumulative mastery of the critical elements is the key to a maturing pattern of skill execution by the end of elementary school physical education. Depth of learning experiences with focused practice provides the maturing skill pattern; breadth is provided by varying environmental contexts and combining skills with other skills and movement concepts. Depth and breadth at the elementary level yield learners prepared for the *application* stage of middle school physical education.

The outcomes for Standard 3 focus on fitness knowledge, engagement in physical activity and assessment. The emphasis of fitness for children in elementary school is fitness within the curriculum of physical education, not formal exercises. Fitness assessment begins in grade 4 and the design of a personalized fitness plan begins in grade 5. The groundwork for Standards 4 and 5 begins in elementary school, as children learn to accept feedback from teachers and peers, interact positively with others and be responsible for personal behavior in physical activity environments. The behaviors and attitudes formed in elementary school exert an extremely strong influence on the behaviors

and attitudes of adolescents and adults in physical activity settings, both in and outside of physical education settings.

Critical Elements

The critical elements are the key components of a motor skill that can be observed, the sum of which results in movement efficiency. It's essential that physical education teachers know the critical elements when providing instructional cues and assessing student progress. The elementary outcomes refer to the critical elements and, in many cases, indicate a particular number of the elements that learners should be able to demonstrate at a particular grade level. To assist teachers in implementing these outcomes, the critical elements of selected fundamental motor skills are presented here, along with illustrations.

The critical elements are arranged by categories (locomotor and manipulative) and are listed in the order in which they first appear in Table 3.1.

Locomotor skills:

- Running
- Jumping and landing for distance (horizontal plane)
- Jumping and landing for height (vertical plane)

Manipulative skills:

- Throwing (underhand pattern)
- Throwing (overhand pattern)
- Catching
- Dribbling
- Kicking
- **Volleying** (underhand)
- Volleying (overhead)
- **Striking** with short implement
- Striking with long implement

RUNNING

- Arm–leg opposition throughout running action.
- Toes point forward.
- Foot lands heel to toe.
- Arms swing forward and backward—no crossing of midline.
- Trunk leans slightly forward.

JUMPING AND LANDING FOR DISTANCE (HORIZONTAL PLANE)

- Arms back and knees bend in preparation for jumping action.
- Arms extend forward as body propels forward.
- Body extends and stretches slightly upward while in flight.
- Hips, knees and ankles bend on landing.
- Shoulders, knees and ankles align for balance after landing.

JUMPING AND LANDING FOR HEIGHT (VERTICAL PLANE)

- Hips, knees and ankles bend in preparation for jumping action.
- Arms extend upward as body propels upward.
- Body extends and stretches upward while in flight.
- Hips, knees and ankles bend on landing.
- Shoulders, knees and ankles align for balance after landing.

THROWING (UNDERHAND PATTERN)

- Face target in preparation for throwing action.
- Arm back in preparation for action.
- Step with opposite foot as throwing arm moves forward.
- Release ball between knee and waist level.
- Follow through to target.

THROWING (OVERHAND PATTERN)

- Side to target in preparation for throwing action.
- Arm back and extended, and elbow at shoulder height or slightly above in preparation for action; elbow leads.
- Step with opposite foot as throwing arm moves forward.
- Hip and spine rotate as throwing action is executed.
- Follow through toward target and across body.

CATCHING

- Extend arms outward to reach for ball.
  - Thumbs in for catch above the waist.
  - Thumbs out for catch at or below the waist.
- Watch the ball all the way into the hands.
- Catch with hands only; no cradling against the body.
- Pull the ball into the body as the catch is made.
- Curl the body slightly around the ball.

DRIBBLING

- Knees slightly bent.
- Opposite foot forward when dribbling in self-space.
- Contact ball with finger pads.
- Firm contact with top of ball.
  - Contact slightly behind ball for travel.
  - Ball to side and in front of body for travel.
- Eyes looking "over," not down at, the ball.

KICKING

- Arms extend forward in preparation for kicking action.
- Contact with ball is made directly below center of ball (travel in the air); contact with ball is made directly behind center of ball (travel on the ground).
- Contact the ball with shoelaces or top of foot for kicking action.
- Trunk leans back slightly in preparation for kicking action.
- Follow through with kicking leg extending forward and upward toward target.

VOLLEYING (UNDERHAND)

- Face the target in preparation for the volley.
- Opposite foot forward.
- Flat surface with hand for contact of the ball or volleybird.
- Contact with ball or volleybird between knee and waist level.
- Follow through upward and to the target.

VOLLEYING (OVERHEAD)

- Body aligned and positioned under the ball.
- Knees, arms and ankles bent in preparation for the volley.
- Hands rounded; thumbs and first fingers make triangle (without touching) in preparation.
- Ball contacts only the finger pads; wrists stay firm.
- Arms extended upward on contact; follow through slightly toward target.

STRIKING WITH SHORT IMPLEMENT

- Racket back in preparation for striking.
- Step on opposite foot as contact is made.
- Swing racket or paddle low to high.
- Coil and uncoil the trunk for preparation and execution of the striking action.
- Follow through for completion of the striking action.

STRIKING WITH LONG IMPLEMENT (SIDE-ARM PATTERN)

- Bat up and back in preparation for the striking action.
- Step forward on opposite foot as contact is made.
- Coil and uncoil the trunk for preparation and execution of the striking action.
- Swing the bat on a horizontal plane.
- Wrist uncocks on follow-through for completion of the striking action.

Grade-Level Outcomes for Elementary School (K-Grade 5)

By the end of grade 5, the learner will demonstrate competence in fundamental motor skills and selected combinations of skills; use basic movement concepts in dance, gymnastics and small-sided practice tasks; identify basic health-related fitness concepts; exhibit acceptance of self and others in physical activities; and identify the benefits of a physically active lifestyle. Table 3.1 provides the outcomes for the elementary level. Outcomes reflect the developmental expectations for most children at the grade level. *Swimming skills and water-safety activities should be taught if facilities permit.*

Table 3.1 Elementary School Outcomes (K-Grade 5)

Standard 1. Demonstrates competency in a variety of motor skills and movement patterns.

Standard 1	Kindergarten	Grade 1	Grade 2	Grade 3	Grade 4	Grade 5
Locomotor						
S1.E1 Hopping, galloping, running, sliding skipping, leaping	Performs locomotor skills (hopping, galloping, running, sliding, skipping) while maintaining balance. (S1.E1.K)	Hops, gallops, jogs and slides using a mature pattern. (S1.E1.1)	Skips using a mature pattern. (S1.E1.2)	Leaps using a mature pattern. (S1.E1.3)	Uses various locomotor skills in a variety of small-sided practice tasks, dance and educational gymnastics experiences. (S1.E1.4)	Demonstrates mature patterns of locomotor skills in dynamic small-sided practice tasks, gymnastics and dance. (S1.E1.5a) Combines locomotor and manipulative skills in a variety of small-sided practice tasks in game environments. (S1.E1.5b) Combines traveling with manipulative skills for execution to a target (e.g., scoring in soccer, hockey and basketball). (S1.E1.5c)
S1.E2 Jogging, running	Developmentally appropriate/emerging outcomes first appear in Grade 2.	Developmentally appropriate/emerging outcomes first appear in Grade 2.	Runs with a mature pattern. (S1.E2.2a) Travels showing differentiation between jogging and sprinting. (S1.E2.2b)	Travels showing differentiation between sprinting and running. (S1.E2.3)	Runs for distance using a mature pattern. (S1.E2.4)	Uses appropriate pacing for a variety of running distances. (S1.E2.5)
S1.E3 Jumping & landing, horizontal	Performs jumping & landing actions with balance. (S1.E3.K)	Demonstrates 2 of the 5 critical elements for jumping & landing in a horizontal plane using 2-foot take-offs and landings. (S1.E3.1)	Demonstrates 4 of the 5 critical elements for jumping & landing in a horizontal plane using a variety of 1- and 2-foot take-offs and landings. (S1.E3.2)	Jumps and lands in the horizontal plane using a mature pattern. (S1.E3.3)	Uses spring-and-step takeoffs and landings specific to gymnastics. (S1.E3.4)	Combines jumping and landing patterns with locomotor and manipulative skills in dance, gymnastics and small-sided practice tasks in game environments. (S1.E3.5)

Standard 1	Kindergarten	Grade 1	Grade 2	Grade 3	Grade 4	Grade 5
Locomotor (continued)						
S1.E4 Jumping & landing, vertical	*Refer to S1.E3.K.*	Demonstrates 2 of the 5 critical elements for jumping & landing in a vertical plane. (S1.E4.1)	Demonstrates 4 of the 5 critical elements for jumping & landing in a vertical plane. (S1.E4.2)	Jumps and lands in the vertical plane using a mature pattern. (S1.E4.3)	*Refer to S1.E3.4.*	*Refer to S1.E3.5.*
S1.E5 Dance	Performs locomotor skills in response to teacher-led creative dance. (S1.E5.K)	Combines locomotor and nonlocomotor skills in a teacher-designed dance. (S1.E5.1)	Performs a teacher- and/or student-designed rhythmic activity with correct response to simple rhythms. (S1.E5.2)	Performs teacher-selected and developmentally appropriate dance steps and movement patterns. (S1.E5.3)	Combines locomotor movement patterns and dance steps to create and perform an original dance. (S1.E5.4)	Combines locomotor skills in cultural as well as creative dances (self and group) with correct rhythm and pattern. (S1.E5.5)
S1.E6 Combinations	Developmentally appropriate/emerging outcomes first appear in Grade 3.	Developmentally appropriate/emerging outcomes first appear in Grade 3.	Developmentally appropriate/emerging outcomes first appear in Grade 3.	Performs a sequence of locomotor skills, transitioning from one skill to another smoothly and without hesitation. (S1.E6.3)	Combines traveling with manipulative skills of dribbling, throwing, catching and striking in teacher- and/or student-designed small-sided practice tasks. (S1.E6.4)	Applies skill.
Nonlocomotor (stability)[1]						
S1.E7 Balance	Maintains momentary stillness on different bases of support. (S1.E7.Ka) Forms wide, narrow, curled, and twisted body shapes. (S1.E7.Kb)	Maintains stillness on different bases of support with different body shapes. (S1.E7.1)	Balances on different bases of support, combining levels and shapes. (S1.E7.2a) Balances in an inverted position[1] with stillness and supportive base. (S1.E7.2b)	Balances on different bases of support, demonstrating muscular tension and extensions of free body parts. (S1.E7.3)	Balances on different bases of support on apparatus, demonstrating levels and shapes. (S1.E7.4)	Combines balance and transferring weight in a gymnastics sequence or dance with a partner. (S1.E7.5)
S1.E8 Weight transfer	Developmentally appropriate/emerging outcomes first appear in Grade 1.	Transfers weight from one body part to another in self-space in dance and gymnastics environments. (S1.E8.1)	Transfers weight from feet to different body parts/bases of support for balance and/or travel.[1] (S1.E8.2)	Transfers weight from feet to hands for momentary weight support. (S1.E8.3)	Transfers weight from feet to hands, varying speed and using large extensions (e.g., mule kick, handstand, cartwheel).[i] (S1.E8.4)	Transfers weight in gymnastics and dance environments. (S1.E8.5)
S1.E9 Weight transfer, rolling	Rolls sideways in a narrow body shape. (S1.E9.K)	Rolls with either a narrow or curled body shape. (S1.E9.1)	Rolls in different directions with either a narrow or curled body shape. (S1.E9.2)	Applies skill.	Applies skill.	Applies skill.
S1.E10 Curling & stretching; twisting & bending	Contrasts the actions of curling & stretching. (S1.E10.K)	Demonstrates twisting, curling, bending & stretching actions. (S1.E10.1)	Differentiates among twisting, curling, bending & stretching actions. (S1.E10.2)	Moves into and out of gymnastics balances with curling, twisting & stretching actions. (S1.E10.3)	Moves into and out of balances on apparatus with curling, twisting & stretching actions. (S1.E10.4)	Performs curling, twisting & stretching actions with correct application in dance, gymnastics and small-sided practice tasks in game environments. (S1.E10.5)

[1]Teachers must use differentiated instruction and developmentally appropriate practice tasks for individual learners when presenting transfers of weight from feet to other body parts.

Elementary School-Level Outcomes (K-Grade 5) | 27

Table 3.1 Standard 1 *(Cont.)*

Standard 1	Kindergarten	Grade 1	Grade 2	Grade 3	Grade 4	Grade 5
Nonlocomotor (stability)[1] *(continued)*						
S1.E11 Combinations	*Developmentally appropriate/emerging outcomes first appear in Grade 2.*	*Developmentally appropriate/emerging outcomes first appear in Grade 2.*	Combines balances and transfers into a 3-part sequence (i.e., dance, gymnastics). (S1.E11.2)	Combines locomotor skills and movement concepts (levels, shapes, extensions, pathways, force, time, flow) to create and perform a dance. (S1.E11.3)	Combines locomotor skills and movement concepts (levels, shapes, extensions, pathways, force, time, flow) to create and perform a dance with a partner. (S1.E11.4)	Combines locomotor skills and movement concepts (levels, shapes, extensions, pathways, force, time, flow) to create and perform a dance with a group. (S1.E11.5)
S1.E12 Balance & weight transfers	*Developmentally appropriate/emerging outcomes first appear in Grade 3.*	*Developmentally appropriate/emerging outcomes first appear in Grade 3.*	*Developmentally appropriate/emerging outcomes first appear in Grade 3.*	Combines balance and weight transfers with movement concepts to create and perform a dance. (S1.E12.3)	Combines traveling with balance and weight transfers to create a gymnastics sequence with and without equipment or apparatus. (S1.E12.4)	Combines actions, balances and weight transfers to create a gymnastics sequence with a partner on equipment or apparatus. (S1.E12.5)
Manipulative						
S1.E13 Underhand throw	Throws underhand with opposite foot forward. (S1.E13.K)	Throws underhand, demonstrating 2 of the 5 critical elements of a mature pattern. (S1.E13.1)	Throws underhand using a mature pattern. (S1.E13.2)	Throws underhand to a partner or target with reasonable accuracy. (S1.E13.3)	Applies skill.	Throws underhand using a mature pattern in nondynamic environments (closed skills), with different sizes and types of objects. (S1.E13.5a) Throws underhand to a large target with accuracy. (S1.E13.5b)
S1.E14 Overhand throw	*Developmentally appropriate/emerging outcomes first appear in Grade 2.*	*Developmentally appropriate/emerging outcomes first appear in Grade 2.*	Throws overhand demonstrating 2 of the 5 critical elements of a mature pattern. (S1.E14.2)	Throws overhand, demonstrating 3 of the 5 critical elements of a mature pattern, in nondynamic environments (closed skills), for distance and/or force. (S1.E14.3)	Throws overhand using a mature pattern in a nondynamic environments (closed skills). (S1.E14.4a) Throws overhand to a partner or at a target with accuracy at a reasonable distance. (S1.E14.4b)	Throws overhand using a mature pattern in nondynamic environments (closed skills), with different sizes and types of balls (S1.E14.5a) Throws overhand to large target with accuracy (S1.E14.5b)
S1.E15 Passing with hands	*Developmentally appropriate/emerging outcomes first appear in Grade 4.*	*Developmentally appropriate/emerging outcomes first appear in Grade 4.*	*Developmentally appropriate/emerging outcomes first appear in Grade 4.*	*Developmentally appropriate/emerging outcomes first appear in Grade 4.*	Throws to a moving partner with reasonable accuracy in a nondynamic environment (closed skills). (S1.E15.4)	Throws with accuracy, both partners moving. (S1.E15.5a) Throws with reasonable accuracy in dynamic, small-sided practice tasks (S1.E15.5b)

Standard 1	Kindergarten	Grade 1	Grade 2	Grade 3	Grade 4	Grade 5
Manipulative *(continued)*						
S1.E16 Catching	Drops a ball and catches it before it bounces twice. (S1.E16.Ka) Catches a large ball tossed by a skilled thrower. (S1.E16.Kb)	Catches a soft object from a self-toss before it bounces. (S1.E16.1a) Catches various sizes of balls self-tossed or tossed by a skilled thrower. (S1.E16.1b)	Catches a self-tossed or well-thrown large ball with hands, not trapping or cradling against the body. (S1.E16.2)	Catches a gently tossed hand-size ball from a partner, demonstrating 4 of the 5 critical elements of a mature pattern. (S1.E16.3)	Catches a thrown ball above the head, at chest or waist level, and below the waist using a mature pattern in a nondynamic environment (closed skills). (S1.E16.4)	Catches a batted ball above the head, at chest or waist level, and along the ground using a mature pattern in a nondynamic environment (closed skills). (S1.E16.5a) Catches with accuracy, both partners moving. (S1.E16.5b) Catches with reasonable accuracy in dynamic, small-sided practice tasks. (S1.E16.5c)
S1.E17 Dribbling/ball control with hands	Dribbles a ball with 1 hand, attempting the second contact. (S1.E17.K)	Dribbles continuously in self-space using the preferred hand. (S1.E17.1)	Dribbles in self-space with preferred hand demonstrating a mature pattern. (S1.E17.2a) Dribbles using the preferred hand while walking in general space. (S1.E17.2b)	Dribbles and travels in general space at slow to moderate jogging speed with control of ball and body. (S1.E17.3)	Dribbles in self-space with both the preferred and the nonpreferred hands using a mature pattern. (S1.E17.4a) Dribbles in general space with control of ball and body while increasing and decreasing speed. (S1.E17.4b)	Combines hand dribbling with other skills during 1v1 practice tasks. (S1.E17.5)
S1.E18 Dribbling/ball control with feet	Taps a ball using the inside of the foot, sending it forward. (S1.E18.K)	Taps or dribbles a ball using the inside of the foot while walking in general space. (S1.E18.1)	Dribbles with the feet in general space with control of ball and body. (S1.E18.2)	Dribbles with the feet in general space at slow to moderate jogging speed with control of ball and body. (S1.E18.3)	Dribbles with the feet in general space with control of ball and body while increasing and decreasing speed. (S1.E18.4)	Combines foot dribbling with other skills in 1v1 practice tasks. (S1.E18.5)
S1.E19 Passing & receiving with feet	*Developmentally appropriate/emerging outcomes first appear in Grade 3.*	*Developmentally appropriate/emerging outcomes first appear in Grade 3.*	*Developmentally appropriate/emerging outcomes first appear in Grade 3.*	Passes & receives ball with the insides of the feet to a stationary partner, "giving" on reception before returning the pass. (S1.E19.3)	Passes & receives ball with the insides of the feet to a moving partner in a nondynamic environment (closed skills). (S1.E19.4a) Receives and passes a ball with the outsides and insides of the feet to a stationary partner, "giving" on reception before returning the pass. (S1.E19.4b)	Passes with the feet using a mature pattern as both partners travel. (S1.E19.5a) Receives a pass with the feet using a mature pattern as both partners travel. (S1.E19.5b)

Continued

Table 3.1 Standard 1 *(Cont.)*

Standard 1	Kindergarten	Grade 1	Grade 2	Grade 3	Grade 4	Grade 5
Manipulative *(continued)*						
S1.E20 Dribbling in combination	*Developmentally appropriate/emerging outcomes first appear in Grade 4.*	*Developmentally appropriate/emerging outcomes first appear in Grade 4.*	*Developmentally appropriate/emerging outcomes first appear in Grade 4.*	*Developmentally appropriate/emerging outcomes first appear in Grade 4.*	Dribbles with hands or feet in combination with other skills (e.g., passing, receiving, shooting). (S1.E20.4)	Dribbles with hands or feet with mature patterns in a variety of small-sided game forms. (S1.E20.5)
S1.E21 Kicking	Kicks a stationary ball from a stationary position, demonstrating 2 of the 5 elements of a mature kicking pattern. (S1.E21.K)	Approaches a stationary ball and kicks it forward, demonstrating 2 of the 5 critical elements of a mature pattern. (S1.E21.1)	Uses a continuous running approach and kicks a moving ball, demonstrating 3 of the 5 critical elements of a mature pattern. (S1.E21.2)	Uses a continuous running approach and intentionally performs a kick along the ground and a kick in the air, demonstrating 4 of the 5 critical elements of a mature pattern for each. (S1.E21.3a) Uses a continuous running approach and kicks a stationary ball for accuracy. (S1.E21.3b)	Kicks along the ground and in the air, and punts using mature patterns. (S1.E21.4)	Demonstrates mature patterns of kicking and punting in small-sided practice task environments. (S1.E21.5)
S1.E22 Volley, underhand	Volleys a lightweight object (balloon), sending it upward. (S1.E22.K)	Volleys an object with an open palm, sending it upward. (S1.E22.1)	Volleys an object upward with consecutive hits. (S1.E22.2)	Volleys an object with an underhand or sidearm striking pattern, sending it forward over a net, to the wall or over a line to a partner, while demonstrating 4 of the 5 critical elements of a mature pattern. (S1.E22.3)	Volleys underhand using a mature pattern in a dynamic environment (e.g., 2 square, 4 square, handball). (S1.E22.4)	Applies skill.
S1.E23 Volley, overhead	*Developmentally appropriate/emerging outcomes first appear in Grade 4.*	*Developmentally appropriate/emerging outcomes first appear in Grade 4.*	*Developmentally appropriate/emerging outcomes first appear in Grade 4.*	*Developmentally appropriate/emerging outcomes first appear in Grade 4.*	Volleys a ball with a two-hand overhead pattern, sending it upward, demonstrating 4 of the 5 critical elements of a mature pattern. (S1.E23.4)	Volleys a ball using a two-hand pattern, sending it upward to a target. (S1.E23.5)
S1.E24 Striking, short implement	Strikes a lightweight object with a paddle or short-handled racket. (S1.E24.K)	Strikes a ball with a short-handled implement, sending it upward. (S1.E24.1)	Strikes an object upward with a short-handled implement, using consecutive hits. (S1.E24.2)	Strikes an object with a short-handled implement, sending it forward over a low net or to a wall. (S1.E24.3a) Strikes an object with a short-handled implement while demonstrating 3 of the 5 critical elements of a mature pattern. (S1.E24.3b)	Strikes an object with a short-handled implement while demonstrating a mature pattern. (S1.E24.4a) Strikes an object with a short-handled implement, alternating hits with a partner over a low net or against a wall. (S1.E24.4b)	Strikes an object consecutively, with a partner, using a short-handled implement, over a net or against a wall, in either a competitive or cooperative game environment. (S1.E24.5)

Standard 1	Kindergarten	Grade 1	Grade 2	Grade 3	Grade 4	Grade 5
Manipulative *(continued)*						
S1.E25 Striking, long implement	*Developmentally appropriate/emerging outcomes first appear in Grade 2.*	*Developmentally appropriate/emerging outcomes first appear in Grade 2.*	Strikes a ball off a tee or cone with a bat using correct grip and side orientation/proper body orientation. (S1.E25.2)	Strikes a ball with a long-handled implement (e.g., hockey stick, bat, golf club), sending it forward, while using proper grip for the implement. Note: Use batting tee or ball tossed by teacher for batting. (S1.E25.3)	Strikes an object with a long-handled implement (e.g., hockey stick, golf club, bat, tennis or badminton racket) while demonstrating 3 of the 5 critical elements of a mature pattern for the implement (grip, stance, body orientation, swing plane, and follow-through). (S1.E25.4)	Strikes a pitched ball with a bat using a mature pattern. (S1.E25.5a) Combines striking with a long implement (e.g., bat, hockey stick) with receiving and traveling skills in a small-sided game. (S1.E25.5b)
S1.E26 In combination with locomotor	*Developmentally appropriate/emerging outcomes first appear in Grade 4.*	*Developmentally appropriate/emerging outcomes first appear in Grade 4.*	*Developmentally appropriate/emerging outcomes first appear in Grade 4.*	*Developmentally appropriate/emerging outcomes first appear in Grade 4.*	Combines traveling with the manipulative skills of dribbling, throwing, catching and striking in teacher- and/or student-designed small-sided practice-task environments. (S1.E26.4)	Combines manipulative skills and traveling for execution to a target (e.g., scoring in soccer, hockey, and basketball). (S1.E26.5)
S1.E27 Jumping rope	Executes a single jump with self-turned rope. (S1.E27.Ka) Jumps a long rope with teacher-assisted turning. (S1.E27.Kb)	Jumps forward or backward consecutively using a self-turned rope. (S1.E27.1a) Jumps a long rope up to 5 times consecutively with teacher-assisted turning. (S1.E27.1b)	Jumps a self-turned rope consecutively forward and backward with a mature pattern. (S1.E27.2a) Jumps a long rope 5 times consecutively with student turners. (S1.E27.2b)	Performs intermediate jump-rope skills (e.g., a variety of tricks, running in & out of long rope) for both long and short ropes. (S1.E27.3)	Creates a jump-rope routine with either a short or long rope. (S1.E27.4)	Creates a jump-rope routine with a partner using either a short or long rope. (S1.E27.5)

Standard 2. Applies knowledge of concepts, principles, strategies and tactics related to movement and performance.

Standard 2	Kindergarten	Grade 1	Grade 2	Grade 3	Grade 4	Grade 5
Movement concepts						
S2.E1 Space	Differentiates between movement in personal (self-space) and general space. (S2.E1.Ka) Moves in personal space to a rhythm. (S2.E1.Kb)	Moves in self-space and general space in response to designated beats/rhythms. (S2.E1.1)	Combines locomotor skills in general space to a rhythm. (S2.E1.2)	Recognizes the concept of open spaces in a movement context. (S2.E1.3)	Applies the concept of open spaces to combination skills involving traveling (e.g., dribbling and traveling). (S2.E1.4a) Applies the concept of closing spaces in small-sided practice tasks. (S2.E1.4b) Dribbles in general space with changes in direction and speed. (S2.E1.4c)	Combines spatial concepts with locomotor and nonlocomotor movements for small groups in gymnastics, dance and games environments. (S2.E1.5)
S2.E2 Pathways, shapes, levels	Travels in 3 different pathways. (S2.E2.K)	Travels demonstrating low, middle and high levels. (S2.E2.1a) Travels demonstrating a variety of relationships with objects (e.g., over, under, around, through). (S2.E2.1b)	Combines shapes, levels and pathways into simple travel, dance and gymnastics sequences.ⁱⁱ (S2.E2.2)	Recognizes locomotor skills specific to a wide variety of physical activities. (S2.E2.3)	Combines movement concepts with skills in small-sided practice tasks, gymnastics and dance environments. (S2.E2.4)	Combines movement concepts with skills in small-sided practice tasks in game environments, gymnastics and dance with self-direction. (S2.E2.5)
S2.E3 Speed, direction, force	Travels in general space with different speeds. (S2.E3.K)	Differentiates between fast and slow speeds. (S2.E3.1a) Differentiates between strong and light force. (S2.E3.1b)	Varies time and force with gradual increases and decreases. (S2.E3.2)	Combines movement concepts (direction, levels, force, time) with skills as directed by the teacher. (S2.E3.3)	Applies the movement concepts of speed, endurance and pacing for running. (S2.E3.4a) Applies the concepts of direction and force when striking an object with a short-handled implement, sending it toward a designated target. (S2.E3.4b)	Applies movement concepts to strategy in game situations. (S2.E3.5a) Applies the concepts of direction and force to strike an object with a long-handled implement. (S2.E3.5b) Analyzes movement situations and applies movement concepts (e.g., force, direction, speed, pathways, extensions) in small-sided practice tasks in game environments, dance and gymnastics. (S2.E3.5c)

Standard 2	Kindergarten	Grade 1	Grade 2	Grade 3	Grade 4	Grade 5
Movement concepts *(continued)*						
S2.E4 Alignment & muscular tension	*Developmentally appropriate/emerging outcomes first appear in Grade 3.*	*Developmentally appropriate/emerging outcomes first appear in Grade 3.*	*Developmentally appropriate/emerging outcomes first appear in Grade 3.*	Employs the concept of alignment in gymnastics and dance. (S2.E4.3a) Employs the concept of muscular tension with balance in gymnastics and dance. (S2.E4.3b)	Applies skill.	Applies skill.
S2.E5 Strategies & tactics	*Developmentally appropriate/emerging outcomes first appear in Grade 3.*	*Developmentally appropriate/emerging outcomes first appear in Grade 3.*	*Developmentally appropriate/emerging outcomes first appear in Grade 3.*	Applies simple strategies & tactics in chasing activities. (S2.E5.3a) Applies simple strategies in fleeing activities. (S2.E5.3b)	Applies simple offensive strategies & tactics in chasing & fleeing activities. (S2.E5.4a) Applies simple defensive strategies & tactics in chasing and fleeing activities. (S2.E5.4b) Recognizes the types of kicks needed for different games & sports situations. (S2.E5.4c)	Applies basic offensive and defensive strategies & tactics in invasion small-sided practice tasks. (S2.E5.5a) Applies basic offensive and defensive strategies & tactics in net/wall small-sided practice tasks. (S2.E5.5b) Recognizes the type of throw, volley or striking action needed for different games & sports situations. (S2.E5.5c)

Standard 3. Demonstrates the knowledge and skills to achieve and maintain a health-enhancing level of physical activity and fitness.

Standard 3	Kindergarten	Grade 1	Grade 2	Grade 3	Grade 4	Grade 5
Physical activity knowledge						
S3.E1	Identifies active-play opportunities outside physical education class. (S3.E1.K)	Discusses the benefits of being active and exercising and/or playing. (S3.E1.1)	Describes large-motor and/or manipulative physical activities for participation outside physical education class (e.g., before and after school, at home, at the park, with friends, with the family). (S3.E1.2)	Charts participation in physical activities outside physical education class. (S3.E1.3a) Identifies physical activity benefits as a way to become healthier. (S3.E1.3b)	Analyzes opportunities for participating in physical activity outside physical education class. (S3.E1.4)	Charts and analyzes physical activity outside physical education class for fitness benefits of activities. (S3.E1.5)
Engages in physical activity						
S3.E2	Actively participates in physical education class. (S3.E2.K)	Actively engages in physical education class. (S3.E2.1)	Actively engages in physical education class in response to instruction and practice. (S3.E2.2)	Engages in the activities of physical education class without teacher prompting. (S3.E2.3)	Actively engages in the activities of physical education class, both teacher-directed and independent. (S3.E2.4)	Actively engages in all the activities of physical education. (S3.E2.5)
Fitness knowledge						
S3.E3	Recognizes that when you move fast, your heart beats faster and you breathe faster.[iii] (S3.E3.K)	Identifies the heart as a muscle that grows stronger with exercise, play, and physical activity. (S3.E3.1)	Recognizes the use of the body as resistance (e.g., holds body in plank position, animal walks)[iv] for developing strength. (S3.E3.2a) Identifies physical activities that contribute to fitness. (S3.E3.2b)	Describes the concept of fitness and provides examples of physical activity to enhance fitness. (S3.E3.3)	Identifies the components of health-related fitness.[v] (S3.E3.4)	Differentiates between skill-related and health-related fitness.[vi] (S3.E3.5)
S3.E4	*Developmentally appropriate/emerging outcomes first appear in Grade 3.*	*Developmentally appropriate/emerging outcomes first appear in Grade 3.*	*Developmentally appropriate/emerging outcomes first appear in Grade 3.*	Recognizes the importance of warm-up & cool-down relative to vigorous physical activity. (S3.E4.3)	Demonstrates warm-up & cool-down relative to the cardiorespiratory fitness assessment. (S3.E4.4)	Identifies the need for warm-up & cool-down relative to various physical activities. (S3.E4.5)

Standard 3	Kindergarten	Grade 1	Grade 2	Grade 3	Grade 4	Grade 5
Assessment & program planning						
S3.E5	*Developmentally appropriate/emerging outcomes first appear in Grade 3.*	*Developmentally appropriate/emerging outcomes first appear in Grade 3.*	*Developmentally appropriate/emerging outcomes first appear in Grade 3.*	Demonstrates, with teacher direction, the health-related fitness components. (S3.E5.3)	Completes fitness assessments (pre- & post-). (S3.E5.4a) Identifies areas of needed remediation from personal test and, with teacher assistance, identifies strategies for progress in those areas. (S3.E5.4b)	Analyzes results of fitness assessment (pre- & post-), comparing results with fitness components for good health. (S3.E5.5a) Designs a fitness plan to address ways to use physical activity to enhance fitness. (S3.E5.5b)
S3.E6 Nutrition	Recognizes that food provides energy for physical activity. (S3.E6.K)	Differentiates between healthy and unhealthy foods. (S3.E6.1)	Recognizes the "good health balance" of nutrition and physical activity. (S3.E6.2)	Identifies foods that are beneficial for before and after physical activity. (S3.E6.3)	Discusses the importance of hydration and hydration choices relative to physical activities. (S3.E6.4)	Analyzes the impact of food choices relative to physical activity, youth sports & personal health. (S3.E6.5)

Standard 4. Exhibits responsible personal and social behavior that respects self and others.

Standard 4	Kindergarten	Grade 1	Grade 2	Grade 3	Grade 4	Grade 5
Personal responsibility						
S4.E1	Follows directions in group settings (e.g., safe behaviors, following rules, taking turns). (S4.E1.K)	Accepts personal responsibility by using equipment and space appropriately. (S4.E1.1)	Practices skills with minimal teacher prompting. (S4.E1.2)	Exhibits personal responsibility in teacher-directed activities. (S4.E1.3)	Exhibits responsible behavior in independent group situations. (S4.E1.4)	Engages in physical activity with responsible interpersonal behavior (e.g., peer to peer, student to teacher, student to referee). (S4.E1.5)
S4.E2	Acknowledges responsibility for behavior when prompted. (S4.E2.K)	Follows the rules & parameters of the learning environment. (S4.E2.1)	Accepts responsibility for class protocols with behavior and performance actions. (S4.E2.2)	Works independently for extended periods of time. (S4.E2.3)	Reflects on personal social behavior in physical activity. (S4.E2.4)	Participates with responsible personal behavior in a variety of physical activity contexts, environments, and facilities. (S4.E2.5a) Exhibits respect for self with appropriate behavior while engaging in physical activity. (S4.E2.5b)
Accepting feedback						
S4.E3	Follows instruction/ directions when prompted. (S4.E3.K)	Responds appropriately to general feedback from the teacher. (S4.E3.1)	Accepts specific corrective feedback from the teacher. (S4.E3.2)	Accepts and implements specific corrective feedback from the teacher. (S4.E3.3)	Listens respectfully to corrective feedback from others (e.g., peers, adults). (S4.E3.4)	Gives corrective feedback respectfully to peers. (S4.E3.5)
Working with others						
S4.E4	Shares equipment and space with others. (S4.E4.K)	Works independently with others in a variety of class environments (e.g., small & large groups). (S4.E4.1)	Works independently with others in partner environments. (S4.E4.2)	Works cooperatively with others. (S4.E4.3a) Praises others for their success in movement performance. (S4.E4.3b)	Praises the movement performance of others both more- and less-skilled. (S4.E4.4a) Accepts players of all skill levels into the physical activity. (S4.E4.4b)	Accepts, recognizes, and actively involves others with both higher and lower skill abilities into physical activities and group projects. (S4.E4.5)
Rules & etiquette						
S4.E5	Recognizes the established protocols for class activities. (S4.E5.K)	Exhibits the established protocols for class activities. (S4.E5.1)	Recognizes the role of rules and etiquette in teacher-designed physical activities. (S4.E5.2)	Recognizes the role of rules and etiquette in physical activity with peers. (S4.E5.3)	Exhibits etiquette and adherence to rules in a variety of physical activities. (S4.E5.4)	Critiques the etiquette involved in rules of various game activities. (S4.E5.5)
Safety						
S4.E6	Follows teacher directions for safe participation and proper use of equipment with minimal reminders. (S4.E6.K)	Follows teacher directions for safe participation and proper use of equipment without teacher reminders. (S4.E6.1)	Works independently and safely in physical education. (S4.E6.2a) Works safely with physical education equipment. (S4.E6.2b)	Works independently and safely in physical activity settings. (S4.E6.3)	Works safely with peers and equipment in physical activity settings. (S4.E6.4)	Applies safety principles with age-appropriate physical activities. (S4.E6.5)

Standard 5. Recognizes the value of physical activity for health, enjoyment, challenge, self-expression and/or social interaction.

Standard 5	Kindergarten	Grade 1	Grade 2	Grade 3	Grade 4	Grade 5
Health						
S5.E1	Recognizes that physical activity is important for good health. (S5.E1.K)	Identifies physical activity as a component of good health. (S5.E1.1)	Recognizes the value of "good health balance." (Refer to S3.E6.2)	Discusses the relationship between physical activity and good health. (S5.E1.3)	Examines the health benefits of participating in physical activity. (S5.E1.4)	Compares the health benefits of participating in selected physical activities. (S5.E1.5)
Challenge						
S5.E2	Acknowledges that some physical activities are challenging/difficult. (S5.E2.K)	Recognizes that challenge in physical activities can lead to success. (S5.E2.1)	Compares physical activities that bring confidence and challenge. (S5.E2.2)	Discusses the challenge that comes from learning a new physical activity. (S5.E2.3)	Rates the enjoyment of participating in challenging and mastered physical activities. (S5.E2.4)	Expresses (via written essay, visual art, creative dance) the enjoyment and/or challenge of participating in a favorite physical activity. (S5.E2.5)
Self-expression & enjoyment						
S5.E3	Identifies physical activities that are enjoyable.[vii] (S5.E3.Ka) Discusses the enjoyment of playing with friends. (S5.E3.Kb)	Describes positive feelings that result from participating in physical activities. (S5.E3.1a) Discusses personal reasons (i.e., the "why") for enjoying physical activities. (S5.E3.1b)	Identifies physical activities that provide self-expression (e.g., dance, gymnastics routines, practice tasks in game environments). (S5.E3.2)	Reflects on the reasons for enjoying selected physical activities. (S5.E3.3)	Ranks the enjoyment of participating in different physical activities. (S5.E3.4)	Analyzes different physical activities for enjoyment and challenge, identifying reasons for a positive or negative response. (S5.E3.5)
S5.E4 Social interaction	*Developmentally appropriate/emerging outcomes first appear in Grade 3.*	*Developmentally appropriate/emerging outcomes first appear in Grade 3.*	*Developmentally appropriate/emerging outcomes first appear in Grade 3.*	Describes the positive social interactions that come when engaged with others in physical activity. (S5.E4.3)	Describes & compares the positive social interactions when engaged in partner, small-group and large-group physical activities. (S5.E4.4)	Describes the social benefits gained from participating in physical activity (e.g., recess, youth sport). (S5.E4.5)

[i]NASPE, 1992, p. 12.

[ii]Ibid., p. 11.

[iii]NASPE, 2012, p. 14.

[iv]Ibid., p. 6.

[v]Ibid., p. 16.

[vi]Ibid., p 17.

[vii]Ibid., p. 19.

Chapter 4

Middle School-Level Outcomes (Grades 6-8)

Middle school outcomes align with characteristics of the application stage in motor development, which coincides with the onset of puberty and many physical and intellectual changes (Gallahue et al., 2012). Around age 11, learners enter Piaget's fourth level of intellectual development (formal operations), which continues through adulthood. This advancement enables middle school students to deal with abstract ideas such as third-party perspective; to problem solve and develop hypotheses; and to ponder their future (Haibach, Reid, & Collier, 2011). With these increases in cognitive development, learners then have the intellectual ability to apply fundamental motor skills and concepts in varying environmental contexts. Middle school students are ready to become more sophisticated game players, which is reflected by the emphasis on tactics and strategies in the outcomes in this chapter (Standard 2). They also gain the ability to set long-term goals and systematically explore ways of meeting those goals (Haibach et al., 2011). Standard 3 addresses these changes by promoting the planning and implementing of self-selected fitness and physical activity goals.

Gender differences become more prevalent in middle school because of physical changes associated with puberty. Uneven rates of physical maturation and the appearance of secondary sex characteristics can lead to self-consciousness and awkwardness among peers (Haibach et al., 2011). Once they enter puberty, boys begin to gain a strength and size advantage over girls that continues through adulthood. Girls, who once were on equal footing with boys physically, begin to lose ground in activities in which strength, speed and size matter. It's not surprising that several researchers have found that students prefer a single-sex physical education environment as they negotiate the middle school years (Derry, 2002; Greenwood, Stillwell, & Byars, 2001).

In addition, girls and lower-performing students begin to show lower levels of, and interest in, physical activity. Some researchers (Bevans et al., 2010; Garn, Cothran, et al., 2011; Hill & Hannon, 2008; Ntoumanis et al., 2004; Treasure & Roberts, 2001; Zhang et al., 2011) associate these changes with the focus on competitive large-group activities in which more-skilled players dominate. These game situations leave little time for skill development. Students cite a preference for a mastery climate, where the focus is on individual improvement in small-group activities coupled with challenging tasks (Bernstein et al., 2011; Bevans et al., 2010; Gao et al., 2011; Garn, Ware, et al., 2011; Haerens et al., 2010; Hamilton & White, 2008; Ommundsen, 2006; Smith & St. Pierre, 2009; Treasure & Roberts, 2001; Zhang et al., 2011). Standards 1 and 2 address concerns expressed by middle school students through a focus on skill acquisition, small-group learning experiences, and progressive and sequential instruction.

The middle school years also are a time when peer influence supplants that of teachers and parents. Demonstrating independence from parents and gaining social acceptance from peers are important to students. Social acceptance from peers, though, can be undermined in competitive situations in which less-skilled students may feel inadequate (Chepko & Arnold, 2000).

The outcomes in Standards 4 and 5 address the need for social acceptance and growing autonomy by focusing on the ability to cooperate, work with others, accept feedback and make healthy choices. These skills are enhanced by establishing a mastery-oriented climate.

In a mastery-oriented environment, students concentrate on improving and building competency (Barnett et al., 2008a,b; Stodden et al., 2009; Stuart et al., 2005). The focus

becomes sequential and progressive instruction combined with deliberate practice across grade levels that leads to personal competency at the end of the middle school years. The use of small-sided or modified activities, which de-emphasizes competition, also helps to avoid social comparisons and the labeling of students as winners and losers. The instructional climate, then, plays a major role in achieving the middle school outcomes.

Guidance for Using Middle School Outcomes

At the application stage (Gallahue et al., 2012), students have the ability to integrate learning and apply knowledge and skill. That allows teachers to create practice tasks and modify activities that address outcomes from more than one standard. In developing learning experiences, teachers must find ways to integrate complementary outcomes into the task. Simply teaching a skill out of context or delivering facts to students is not effective and fails to account for students' developmental levels. Students need learning experiences that engage them in the physical tasks while challenging them intellectually. This integrated approach is evident in the "teaching games for understanding" (TGFU) model (Griffin & Butler, 2005).

The TGFU model (Griffin & Butler, 2005) advocates that skill practice occurs in the context of game play. While Standard 1 identifies specific skills to create open space in an invasion game, the intent is not to practice those skills in isolation. Learning experiences should integrate the application of skills into the practice task (Standard 2) and allow students to discover the how, when and why of the tactic or strategy. Teachers must incorporate skill practice into learning experiences that develop decision making, allow students to execute skills within a game-like context and promote problem solving.

Teachers have many opportunities for integrating outcomes from Standards 3, 4 and 5. Implicit in meeting the Standard 3 outcome of designing and implementing a program to improve levels of health-related fitness (S3.M16) is the knowledge of the five components and their connection to physical and mental health (S5.M1) from Standard 5. Students could not evaluate the plan without addressing the outcome under Standard 4, which is specific to using effective self-monitoring skills (S4.M2). Teachers should not view the outcomes as discrete tasks taught in isolation but rather as a coordinated process that allows students to apply knowledge and skills across standards.

Embedded in many learning experiences will be opportunities for teachers to "teach to" and "address" outcomes under Standards 3 and 4. Most learning experiences require students to be physically active, thereby creating a multitude of chances to address physical activity and fitness outcomes under Standard 3. Opportunities also are available to address responsible personal and social behaviors in any practice tasks requiring learners to work with a partner or small group. These openings are embedded in learning experiences based on the essential elements of the task. To be successful in the practice task for an invasion game, students must demonstrate cooperation skills or accept differences among classmates (S4.M4). Teachers must find occasions to address these embedded outcomes within practice tasks.

Another example is the use of peer assessments. While the assessment focuses on the effective application of skills and tactics (Standards 1 and 2) or attainment of a physical activity goal (Standard 3), providing feedback to peers is linked directly to Standard 4. Similarly, while giving feedback on the effectiveness of game play or meeting a physical activity goal, the need to encourage classmates and be inclusive can be addressed (also Standard 4).

Teachers must consider what outcome is "embedded" and teach to that outcome. Creating learning experiences that address multiple outcomes is essential to maximizing learning and student engagement during middle school.

The middle school outcomes differ from the elementary outcomes in their emphasis on **applying** skills and knowledge and using activity categories,

which are continued into the high school level. The categories of dance and rhythm, games and sports, outdoor pursuits, individual-performance activities and aquatics organize outcomes under Standards 1 and 2. Due to the introduction of formal tactics and strategies in middle school, the emphasis is on games and sports at this level. It's essential, however, to include a wider variety of physical activity in the curriculum to support interests of all students and address the breadth of the outcomes.

The games and sports category is further broken down into target, invasion, fielding/striking and net/wall games. That allows practitioners to teach for transfer of skills and concepts across grade levels and categories. For example, catching is taught in all three grade levels, but the environmental context becomes more complex each year. The use of categories has the added advantage of allowing multiple exposures to a category of activities without repeating the same activity or unit each year. If soccer is taught in grade 6, different invasion games are taught in grades 7 and 8. Teachers teach for transfer of skills and concepts common to the category. Finally, the unit length must be suf-ficient to allow for skill acquisition. Competency requires meaningful practice, not just a few exposures. While it's difficult to set a standard length, teachers should consider unit lengths of at least eight lessons for most activities.

Grade-Level Outcomes for Middle School (Grades 6-8)

By the end of grade 8, the learner will apply tactics and strategies to modified game play, demonstrate fundamental motor skills in a variety of contexts, design and implement a health-enhancing fitness program, participate in self-selected physical activity, cooperate with and encourage classmates, accept individual differences and demonstrate inclusive behaviors, and engage in physical activity for enjoyment and self-expression. Table 4.1 provides the outcomes for the middle school level. Outcomes reflect the developmental expectations for most children at the grade level. Swimming skills and water-safety activities should be taught if facilities permit.

Table 4.1 Middle School Outcomes (Grades 6-8)

Standard 1. Demonstrates competency in a variety of motor skills and movement patterns.

Standard 1	Grade 6	Grade 7	Grade 8
Dance & rhythms			
S1.M1	Demonstrates correct rhythm and pattern for 1 of the following dance forms: folk, social, creative, line or world dance. (S1.M1.6)	Demonstrates correct rhythm and pattern for a different dance form from among folk, social, creative, line and world dance. (S1.M1.7)	Exhibits command of rhythm and timing by creating a movement sequence to music as an individual or in a group. (S1.M1.8)
Games & sports: Invasion & field games			
S1.M2 Throwing	Throws with a mature pattern for distance or power appropriate to the practice task (e.g., distance = outfield to home plate; power = 2nd base to 1st base). (S1.M2.6)	Throws with a mature pattern for distance or power appropriate to the activity in a dynamic environment. (S1.M2.7)	Throws with a mature pattern for distance or power appropriate to the activity during small-sided game play. (S1.M2.8)
S1.M3 Catching	Catches with a mature pattern from a variety of trajectories using different objects in varying practice tasks. (S1.M3.6)	Catches with a mature pattern from a variety of trajectories using different objects in small-sided game play. (S1.M3.7)	Catches using an implement in a dynamic environment or modified game play. (S1.M3.8)
Games & sports: Invasion games			
S1.M4 Passing & receiving	Passes and receives with hands in combination with locomotor patterns of running and change of direction & speed with competency in modified invasion games such as basketball, flag football, speedball, or team handball. (S1.M4.6)	Passes and receives with feet in combination with locomotor patterns of running and change of direction and speed with competency in modified invasion games such as soccer or speedball. (S1.M4.7)	Passes and receives with an implement in combination with locomotor patterns of running and change of direction, speed and/or level with competency in modified invasion games such as lacrosse or hockey (floor, field, ice). (S1.M4.8)

Standard 1	Grade 6	Grade 7	Grade 8
Games & sports: Invasion games *(continued)*			
S1.M5 Passing & receiving	Throws, while stationary, a leading pass to a moving receiver. (S1.M5.6)	Throws, while moving, a leading pass to a moving receiver. (S1.M5.7)	Throws a lead pass to a moving partner off a dribble or pass. (S1.M5.8)
S1.M6 Offensive skills	Performs pivots, fakes and jab steps designed to create open space during practice tasks. (S1.M6.6)	Executes at least 1 of the following designed to create open space during small-sided game play: pivots, fakes, jab steps. (S1.M6.7)	Executes at least 2 of the following to create open space during modified game play: pivots, fakes, jab steps, screens. (S1.M6.8)
S1.M7 Offensive skills	Performs the following offensive skills without defensive pressure: pivot, give & go, and fakes. (S1.M7.6)	Performs the following offensive skills with defensive pressure: pivot, give & go, and fakes. (S1.M7.7)	Executes the following offensive skills during small-sided game play: pivot, give & go, and fakes. (S1.M7.8)
S1.M8 Dribbling/ball control	Dribbles with dominant hand using a change of speed and direction in a variety of practice tasks. (S1.M8.6)	Dribbles with dominant and nondominant hands using a change of speed and direction in a variety of practice tasks. (S1.M8.7)	Dribbles with dominant and nondominant hands using a change of speed and direction in small-sided game play. (S1.M8.8)
S1.M9 Dribbling/ball control	Foot-dribbles or dribbles with an implement with control, changing speed and direction in a variety of practice tasks. (S1.M9.6)	Foot-dribbles or dribbles with an implement combined with passing in a variety of practice tasks. (S1.M9.7)	Foot-dribbles or dribbles with an implement with control, changing speed and direction during small-sided game play. (S1.M9.8)
S1.M10 Shooting on goal	Shoots on goal with power in a dynamic environment as appropriate to the activity. (S1.M10.6)	Shoots on goal with power and accuracy in small-sided game play. (S1.M10.7)	Shoots on goal with a long-handled implement for power and accuracy in modified invasion games such as hockey (floor, field, ice) or lacrosse. (S1.M10.8)
S1.M11 Defensive skills	Maintains defensive ready position with weight on balls of feet, arms extended, and eyes on midsection of the offensive player. (S1.M11.6)	Slides in all directions while on defense without crossing feet. (S1.M11.7)	Drop-steps in the direction of the pass during player-to-player defense. (S1.M11.8)
Games & sports: Net/wall games			
S1.M12 Serving	Performs a legal underhand serve with control for net/wall games such as badminton, volleyball or pickleball. (S1.M12.6)	Executes consistently (at least 70% of the time) a legal underhand serve to a predetermined target for net/wall games such as badminton, volleyball or pickleball. (S1.M12.7)	Executes consistently (at least 70% of the time) a legal underhand serve for distance and accuracy for net/wall games such as badminton, volleyball or pickleball. (S1.M12.8)
S1.M13 Striking	Strikes with a mature overhand pattern in a nondynamic environment (closed skills) for net/wall games such as volleyball, handball, badminton or tennis. (S1.M13.6)	Strikes with a mature overhand pattern in a dynamic environment for net/wall games such as volleyball, handball, badminton or tennis. (S1.M13.7)	Strikes with a mature overhand pattern in a modified game for net/wall games such as volleyball, handball, badminton or tennis. (S1.M13.8)
S1.M14 Forehand & backhand	Demonstrates the mature form of the forehand and backhand strokes with a short-handled implement in net games such as paddleball, pickleball or short-handled racket tennis. (S1.M14.6)	Demonstrates the mature form of forehand and backhand strokes with a long-handled implement in net games such as badminton or tennis. (S1.M14.7)	Demonstrates the mature form of forehand and backhand strokes with a short- or long-handled implement with power and accuracy in net games such as pickleball, tennis, badminton or paddleball. (S1.M14.8)
S1.M15 Weight transfer	Transfers weight with correct timing for the striking pattern. (S1.M15.6)	Transfers weight with correct timing using low-to-high striking pattern with a short-handled implement on the forehand side. (S1.M15.7)	Transfers weight with correct timing using low-to-high striking pattern with a long-handled implement on the backhand side. (S1.M15.8)
S1.M16 Volley	Forehand volleys with a mature form and control using a short-handled implement. (S1.M16.6)	Forehand and backhand volleys with a mature form and control using a short-handled implement. (S1.M16.7)	Forehand and backhand volleys with a mature form and control using a short-handled implement during modified game play. (S1.M16.8)
S1.M17 Two-hand volley	Two-hand-volleys with control in a variety of practice tasks. (S1.M17.6)	Two-hand-volleys with control in a dynamic environment. (S1.M17.7)	Two-hand-volleys with control in a small-sided game. (S1.M17.8)

Continued

Table 4.1 Standard 1 *(Cont.)*

Standard 1	Grade 6	Grade 7	Grade 8
Games & sports: Net/wall games *(continued)*			
S1.M18 Underhand throw	Demonstrates a mature underhand pattern for a modified target game such as bowling, bocce or horseshoes. (S1.M18.6)	Executes consistently (70% of the time) a mature underhand pattern for target games such as bowling, bocce, or horseshoes. (S1.M18.7)	Performs consistently (70% of the time) a mature underhand pattern with accuracy and control for 1 target game such as bowling or bocce. (S1.M18.8)
S1.M19 Striking	Strikes, with an implement, a stationary object for accuracy in activities such as croquet, shuffleboard or golf. (S1.M19.6)	Strikes, with an implement, a stationary object for accuracy and distance in activities such as croquet, shuffleboard or golf. (S1.M19.7)	Strikes, with an implement, a stationary object for accuracy and power in such activities as croquet, shuffleboard or golf. (S1.M19.8)
Games & sports: Fielding/striking games			
S1.M20 Striking	Strikes a pitched ball with an implement with force in a variety of practice tasks. (S1.M20.6)	Strikes a pitched ball with an implement to open space in a variety of practice tasks. (S1.M20.7)	Strikes a pitched ball with an implement for power to open space in a variety of small-sided games. (S1.M20.8)
S1.M21 Catching	Catches, with a mature pattern, from different trajectories using a variety of objects in a varying practice tasks. (S1.M21.6)	Catches, with a mature pattern, from different trajectories using a variety of objects in small-sided game play. (S1.M21.7)	Catches, using an implement, from different trajectories and speeds in a dynamic environment or modified game play. (S1.M21.8)
Outdoor pursuits			
S1.M22 (See end of chapter for examples)	Demonstrates correct technique for basic skills in 1 self-selected outdoor activity. (S1.M22.6)	Demonstrates correct technique for a variety of skills in 1 self-selected outdoor activity. (S1.M22.7)	Demonstrates correct technique for basic skills in at least 2 self-selected outdoor activities. (S1.M22.8)
Aquatics			
S1.M23	Preferably taught at elementary or secondary levels. However, availability of facilities might dictate when swimming and water safety are offered in the curriculum.		
Individual-performance activities			
S1.M24 (See end of chapter for examples)	Demonstrates correct technique for basic skills in 1 self-selected individual-performance activity. (S1.M25.6)	Demonstrates correct technique for a variety of skills in 1 self-selected individual-performance activity. (S1.M25.7)	Demonstrates correct technique for basic skills in at least 2 self-selected individual-performance activities. (S1.M25.8)

Standard 2. Applies knowledge of concepts, principles, strategies and tactics related to movement and performance.

Standard 2	Grade 6	Grade 7	Grade 8
Games & sports*: Invasion games			
S2.M1 Creating space with movement	Creates open space by using locomotor movements (e.g., walking, running, jumping & landing) in combination with movement (e.g., varying pathways; change of speed, direction or pace). (S2.M1.6)	Reduces open space by using locomotor movements (e.g., walking, running, jumping & landing, changing size and shape of the body) in combination with movement concepts (e.g., reducing the angle in the space, reducing distance between player and goal). (S2.M1.7)	Opens and closes space during small-sided game play by combining locomotor movements with movement concepts. (S2.M1.8)
S2.M2 Creating space with offensive tactics	Executes at least 1 of the following offensive tactics to create open space: moves to open space without the ball; uses a variety of passes, pivots and fakes; give & go. (S2.M2.6)	Executes at least 2 of the following offensive tactics to create open space: uses a variety of passes, pivots and fakes; give & go. (S2.M2.7)	Executes at least 3 of the following offensive tactics to create open space: moves to create open space on and off the ball; uses a variety of passes, fakes and pathways; give & go. (S2.M2.8)
S2.M3 Creating space using width & length	Creates open space by using the width and length of the field/court on offense. (S2.M3.6)	Creates open space by staying spread on offense, and cutting and passing quickly. (S2.M3.7)	Creates open space by staying spread on offense, cutting and passing quickly, and using fakes off the ball. (S2.M3.8)
Games & sports*: Invasion games			
S2.M4 Reducing space by changing size & shape	Reduces open space on defense by making the body larger and reducing passing angles. (S2.M4.6)	Reduces open space on defense by staying close to the opponent as he/she nears the goal. (S2.M4.7)	Reduces open space on defense by staying on the goal side of the offensive player and reducing the distance to him/her (third-party perspective). (S2.M4.8)
S2.M5 Reducing space using denial	Reduces open space by not allowing the catch (denial) or by allowing the catch but not the return pass. (S2.M5.6)	Reduces open space by not allowing the catch (denial) or anticipating the speed of the object or person for the purpose of interception or deflection. (S2.M5.7)	Reduces open space by not allowing the catch (denial) and anticipating the speed of the object or person for the purpose of interception or deflection. (S2.M5.8)
S2.M6 Transitions	Transitions from offense to defense or defense to offense by recovering quickly. (S2.M6.6)	Transitions from offense to defense or defense to offense by recovering quickly and communicating with teammates. (S2.M6.7)	Transitions from offense to defense or defense to offense by recovering quickly, communicating with teammates and capitalizing on an advantage. (S2.M6.8)
Games & sports: Net/wall games			
S2.M7 Creating space through variation	Creates open space in net/wall games with a short-handled implement by varying force and direction. (S2.M7.6)	Creates open space in net/wall games with a long-handled implement by varying force and direction, and moving opponent from side to side. (S2.M7.7)	Creates open space in net/wall games with either a long- or short-handled implement by varying force or direction or by moving opponent side to side and/or forward and back. (S2.M7.8)
S2.M8 Using tactics & shots	Reduces offensive options for opponents by returning to midcourt position. (S2.M8.6)	Selects offensive shot based on opponent's location (hit where opponent is not). (S2.M8.7)	Varies placement, force and timing of return to prevent anticipation by opponent. (S2.M8.8)
Games & sports: Target games			
S2.M9 Shot selection	Selects appropriate shot and/or club based on location of the object in relation to the target. (S2.M9.6)	Varies the speed and/or trajectory of the shot based on location of the object in relation to the target. (S2.M9.7)	Varies the speed, force and trajectory of the shot based on location of the object in relation to the target. (S2.M9.8)
Games & sports: Fielding/striking games			
S2.M10 Offensive strategies	Identifies open spaces and attempts to strike object into that space. (S2.M10.6)	Uses a variety of shots (e.g., slap & run, bunt, line drive, high arc) to hit to open space. (S2.M10.7)	Identifies sacrifice situations and attempt to advance a teammate. (S2.M10.8)

Continued

Table 4.1 Standard 2 *(Cont.)*

Standard 2	Grade 6	Grade 7	Grade 8
Games & sports: Fielding/striking games *(continued)*			
S2.M11 Reducing space	Identifies the correct defensive play based on the situation (e.g., number of outs). (S2.M11.6)	Selects the correct defensive play based on the situation (e.g., number of outs). (S2.M11.7)	Reduces open spaces in the field by working with teammates to maximize coverage. (S2.M11.8)
Individual-performance activities, dance & rhythms			
S2.M12 Movement concepts	Varies application of force during dance or gymnastic activities. (S2.M12.6)	Identifies and applies Newton's laws of motion to various dance or movement activities. (S2.M12.7)	Describes and applies mechanical advantage(s) for a variety of movement patterns. (S2.M12.8)
Outdoor pursuits			
S2.M13 Movement concepts	Makes appropriate decisions based on the weather, level of difficulty due to conditions or ability to ensure safety of self and others. (S2.M13.6)	Analyzes the situation and makes adjustments to ensure the safety of self and others. (S2.M13.7)	Implements safe protocols in self-selected outdoor activities. (S2.M13.8)

Standard 3. Demonstrates the knowledge and skills to achieve and maintain a health-enhancing level of physical activity and fitness.

Standard 3	Grade 6	Grade 7	Grade 8
Physical activity knowledge			
S3.M1	Describes how being physically active leads to a healthy body. (S3.M1.6)	Identifies barriers related to maintaining a physically active lifestyle and seeks solutions for eliminating those barriers. (S3.M1.7)	Identifies the 5 components of health-related fitness (muscular strength, muscular endurance, flexibility, cardiovascular endurance, body composition) and explains the connections between fitness and overall physical and mental health. (S3.M1.8)
Engages in physical activity			
S3.M2	Participates in self-selected physical activity outside of physical education class. (S3.M2.6)	Participates in a physical activity twice a week outside of physical education class. (S3.M2.7)	Participates in physical activity 3 times a week outside of physical education class. (S3.M2.8)
S3.M3	Participates in a variety of aerobic-fitness activities such as cardio–kick, step aerobics and aerobic dance. (S3.M3.6)	Participates in a variety of strength- and endurance-fitness activities such as Pilates, resistance training, body-weight training and light free-weight training. (S3.M3.7)	Participates in a variety of self-selected aerobic-fitness activities outside of school such as walking, jogging, biking, skating, dancing and swimming. (S3.M3.8)
S3.M4	Participates in a variety of aerobic-fitness activities using technology such as Dance Dance Revolution or Wii Fit. (S3.M4.6)	Participates in a variety of strength- and endurance-fitness activities such as weight or resistance training. (S3.M4.7)	Plans and implements a program of cross-training to include aerobic, strength & endurance and flexibility training. (S3.M4.8)
S3.M5	Participates in a variety of lifetime recreational team sports, outdoor pursuits or dance activities. (S3.M5.6)	Participates in a variety of lifetime dual and individual sports, martial arts or aquatic activities. (S3.M5.7)	Participates in a self-selected lifetime sport, dance, aquatic or outdoor activity outside of the school day. (S3.M5.8)
Fitness knowledge			
S3.M6	Participates in moderate to vigorous aerobic physical activity that includes intermittent or continuous aerobic physical activity of both moderate and vigorous intensity for at least 60 minutes per day. (S3.M6.6)	Participates in moderate to vigorous muscle- and bone-strengthening physical activity at least 3 times a week. (S3.M6.7)	Participates in moderate to vigorous aerobic and/or muscle- and bone-strengthening physical activity for at least 60 minutes per day at least 5 times a week. (S3.M6.8)
S3.M7	Identifies the components of skill-related fitness. (S3.M7.6)	Distinguishes between health-related and skill-related fitness.[i] (S3.M7.7)	Compares and contrasts health-related fitness components.[ii] (S3.M7.8)
S3.M8	Sets and monitors a self-selected physical-activity goal for aerobic and/or muscle- and bone-strengthening activity based on current fitness level. (S3.M8.6)	Adjusts physical activity based on quantity of exercise needed for a minimal health standard and/or optimal functioning based on current fitness level. (S3.M8.7)	Uses available technology to self-monitor quantity of exercise needed for a minimal health standard and/or optimal functioning based on current fitness level. (S3.M8.8)
S3.M9	Employs correct techniques and methods of stretching.[iii] (S3.M9.6)	Describes and demonstrates the difference between dynamic and static stretches.[iv] (S3.M9.7)	Employs a variety of appropriate static-stretching techniques for all major muscle groups. (S3.M9.8)
S3.M10	Differentiates between aerobic and anaerobic capacity and between muscular strength and endurance. (S3.M10.6)	Describes the role of exercise and nutrition in weight management. (S3.M10.7)	Describes the role of flexibility in injury prevention. (S3.M10.8)
S3.M11	Identifies each of the components of the overload principle (FITT formula: frequency, intensity, time & type) for different types of physical activity (aerobic, muscular fitness, and flexibility). (S3.M11.6)	Describes the overload principle (FITT formula)) for different types of physical activity, the training principles on which the formula is based and how the formula and principles affect fitness.[v] (S3.M11.7)	Uses the overload principle (FITT formula) in preparing a personal workout.[vi] (S3.M11.8)

Continued

Table 4.1 Standard 3 *(Cont.)*

Standard 3	Grade 6	Grade 7	Grade 8
Fitness knowledge *(continued)*			
S3.M12	Describes the role of warm-ups and cool-downs before and after physical activity. (S3.M12.6)	Designs a warm-up/ cool-down regimen for a self-selected physical activity. (S3.M12.7)	Designs and implements a warm-up/ cool-down regimen for a self-selected physical activity. (S3.M12.8)
S3.M13	Defines resting heart rate and describes its relationship to aerobic fitness and the Borg Rating of Perceived Exertion (RPE) Scale.[vii] (S3.M13.6)	Defines how the RPE Scale can be used to determine the perception of the work effort or intensity of exercise. (S3.M13.7)	Defines how the RPE Scale can be used to adjust workout intensity during physical activity. (S3.M13.8)
S3.M14	Identifies major muscles used in selected physical activities.[viii] (S3.M14.6)	Describes how muscles pull on bones to create movement in pairs by relaxing and contracting.[ix] (S3.M14.7)	Explains how body systems interact with one another (e.g., blood transports nutrients from the digestive system, oxygen from the respiratory system) during physical activity.[x] (S3.M14.8)
Assessment & program planning			
S3.M15	Designs and implements a program of remediation for any areas of weakness based on the results of health-related fitness assessment. (S3.M15.6)	Designs and implements a program of remediation for 2 areas of weakness based on the results of health-related fitness assessment. (S3.M15.7)	Designs and implements a program of remediation for 3 areas of weakness based on the results of health-related fitness assessment. (S3.M15.8)
S3.M16	Maintains a physical activity log for at least 2 weeks and reflects on activity levels as documented in the log. (S3.M16.6)	Maintains a physical activity and nutrition log for at least 2 weeks and reflects on activity levels and nutrition as documented in the log. (S3.M16.7)	Designs and implements a program to improve levels of health-related fitness and nutrition. (S3.M16.8)
Nutrition			
S3.M17	Identifies foods within each of the basic food groups and selects appropriate servings and portions for his/her age and physical activity levels.[xi] (S3.M17.6)	Develops strategies for balancing healthy food, snacks and water intake, along with daily physical activity.[xii] (S3.M17.7)	Describes the relationship between poor nutrition and health risk factors.[xiii] (S3.M17.8)
Stress management			
S3.M18	Identifies positive and negative results of stress and appropriate ways of dealing with each.[xiv] (S3.M18.6)	Practices strategies for dealing with stress, such as deep breathing, guided visualization, and aerobic exercise.[xv] (S3.M18.7)	Demonstrates basic movements used in other stress-reducing activities, such as yoga and tai chi. (S3.M18.8)

Standard 4. Exhibits responsible personal and social behavior that respects self and others.

Standard 4	Grade 6	Grade 7	Grade 8
Personal responsibility			
S4.M1	Exhibits personal responsibility by using appropriate etiquette, demonstrating respect for facilities, and exhibiting safe behaviors. (S4.M1.6)	Exhibits responsible social behaviors by cooperating with classmates, demonstrating inclusive behaviors, and supporting classmates. (S4.M1.7)	Accepts responsibility for improving one's own levels of physical activity and fitness. (S4.M1.8)
S4.M2	Identifies and uses appropriate strategies to self-reinforce positive fitness behaviors, such as positive self-talk. (S4.M2.6)	Demonstrates both intrinsic and extrinsic motivation by selecting opportunities to participate in physical activity outside of class. (S4.M2.7)	Uses effective self-monitoring skills to incorporate opportunities for physical activity in and outside of school. (S4.M2.8)
Accepting feedback			
S4.M3	Demonstrates self-responsibility by implementing specific corrective feedback to improve performance. (S4.M3.6)	Provides corrective feedback to a peer using teacher-generated guidelines and incorporating appropriate tone and other communication skills. (S4.M3.7)	Provides encouragement and feedback to peers without prompting from the teacher. (S4.M3.8)

Standard 4	Grade 6	Grade 7	Grade 8
Working with others			
S4.M4	Accepts differences among classmates in physical development, maturation, and varying skill levels by providing encouragement and positive feedback. (S4.M4.6)	Demonstrates cooperation skills by establishing rules and guidelines for resolving conflicts. (S4.M4.7)	Responds appropriately to participants' ethical and unethical behavior during physical activity by using rules and guidelines for resolving conflicts. (S4.M4.8)
S4.M5	Cooperates with a small group of classmates during adventure activities, game play, or team-building activities. (S4.M5.6)	Problem solves with a small group of classmates during adventure activities, small-group initiatives, or game play. (S4.M5.7)	Cooperates with multiple classmates on problem-solving initiatives, including adventure activities, large-group initiatives, and game play. (S4.M5.8)
Rules & etiquette			
S4.M6	Identifies the rules and etiquette for physical activities, games and dance activities. (S4.M6.6)	Demonstrates knowledge of rules and etiquette by self-officiating modified physical activities and games or following parameters to create or modify a dance. (S4.M6.7)	Applies rules and etiquette by acting as an official for modified physical activities and games and creating dance routines within a given set of parameters. (S4.M6.8)
Safety			
S4.M7	Uses physical activity and fitness equipment appropriately and safely, with the teacher's guidance. (S4.M7.6)	Independently uses physical activity and exercise equipment appropriately and safely. (S4.M7.7)	Independently uses physical activity and fitness equipment appropriately, and identifies specific safety concerns associated with the activity. (S4.M7.8)

Standard 5. Recognizes the value of physical activity for health, enjoyment, challenge, self-expression and/or social interaction.

Standard 5	Grade 6	Grade 7	Grade 8
Health			
S5.M1	Describes how being physically active leads to a healthy body. (S5.M1.6)	Identifies different types of physical activities and describes how each exerts a positive impact on health. (S5.M1.7)	Identifies the 5 components of health-related fitness (muscular strength, muscular endurance, flexibility, cardiovascular endurance and body composition) and explains the connections between fitness and overall physical and mental health. (S5.M1.8)
S5.M2	Identifies components of physical activity that provide opportunities for reducing stress and for social interaction. (S5.M2.6)	Identifies positive mental and emotional aspects of participating in a variety of physical activities. (S5.M2.7)	Analyzes the empowering consequences of being physical active. (S5.M2.8)
Challenge			
S5.M3	Recognizes individual challenges and copes in a positive way, such as extending effort, asking for help or feedback, or modifying the tasks. (S5.M3.6)	Generates positive strategies such as offering suggestions or assistance, leading or following others and providing possible solutions when faced with a group challenge. (S5.M3.7)	Develops a plan of action and makes appropriate decisions based on that plan when faced with an individual challenge. (S5.M3.8)
Self-expression & enjoyment			
S5.M4	Describes how moving competently in a physical activity setting creates enjoyment. (S5.M4.6)	Identifies why self-selected physical activities create enjoyment. (S5.M4.7)	Discusses how enjoyment could be increased in self-selected physical activities. (S5.M4.8)
S5.M5	Identifies how self-expression and physical activity are related. (S5.M5.6)	Explains the relationship between self-expression and lifelong enjoyment through physical activity. (S5.M5.7)	Identifies and participates in an enjoyable activity that prompts individual self-expression. (S5.M5.8)
Social interaction			
S5.M6	Demonstrates respect for self and others in activities and games by following the rules, encouraging others and playing in the spirit of the game or activity. (S5.M6.6)	Demonstrates the importance of social interaction by helping and encouraging others, avoiding trash talk and providing support to classmates. (S5.M6.7)	Demonstrates respect for self by asking for help and helping others in various physical activities. (S5.M6.8)

*The foundation for this section comes from Griffin and Butler (2005); Griffin, Mitchell and Oslin (2006); and Rovegno and Bandauer (2013).

[i]NASPE, 2012, p. 16.

[ii]Ibid.

[iii]Ibid., p. 7.

[iv]Ibid.

[v]Ibid., p. 17.

[vi]Ibid.

[vii]Ibid., p. 14.

[viii]Ibid., p. 13.

[ix]Ibid.

[x]Ibid.

[xi]Ibid., p. 42.

[xii]Ibid., p. 45.

[xiii]Ibid., p. 40.

[xiv]Ibid., p. 35.

[xv]Ibid.

Operational Definitions of Activity Categories

- **Outdoor pursuits:** The outdoor environment is an important factor in student engagement in the activity. Activities might include but are not limited to recreational boating (e.g., kayaking, canoeing, sailing, rowing); hiking; backpacking; fishing; orienteering or geocaching; ice skating; skateboarding; snow or water skiing; snowboarding; snowshoeing; surfing; bouldering, traversing, or climbing; mountain biking; adventure activities; and ropes courses. Selection of activities depends on the environmental opportunities within the geographical region.

- **Fitness activities:** Activities with a focus on improving or maintaining fitness. Fitness activities might include but are not limited to yoga, Pilates, resistance training, spinning, running, fitness walking, fitness swimming, kickboxing, cardio–kick, Zumba and exergaming.

- **Dance and rhythmic activities:** Activities that focus on dance or rhythms. Dance and rhythmic activities might include but are not limited to dance forms such as creative movement or dance, ballet, modern, ethnic or folk, hip hop, Latin, line, ballroom, social and square.

- **Aquatics:** Might include but are not limited to swimming, diving, synchronized swimming and water polo.

- **Individual-performance activities:** Might include but are not limited to gymnastics, figure skating, track and field, multisport events, in-line skating, wrestling, self-defense and skateboarding.

- **Games and sports:** Includes the games categories of invasion, net/wall, target and fielding/striking.

- **Lifetime activities:** Includes the categories of outdoor pursuits, selected individual-performance activities, aquatics, and net/wall and target games. *Note:* Invasion and fielding/striking games have been excluded from the high school outcomes because these activities require team participation and are less suited to lifelong participation.

Chapter 5

High School-Level Outcomes (Grades 9-12)

The high school physical education years correspond with the lifelong utilization stage of motor development, which begins at about age 14 (Gallahue et al., 2012, p. 55). In this stage, students acquire and hone the specialized physical skills and knowledge they will use in adulthood. The high school outcomes that follow are intended to support the characteristics of this stage by preparing students for a physically active lifestyle and culminating in a physically literate individual. To accomplish that, the student learning outcomes extend the applied skills and knowledge developed in middle school, but with a more concentrated focus on planning and implementing lifetime physical activity goals.

In the lifelong utilization stage, many elements influence specialized skill development. Those elements can include students' competency and perceived competency, their personal interests and the availability of opportunities (Gallahue et al., 2012, p. 55). As research has shown, the importance of competency for continued engagement in physical activity is paramount, with students more likely to be interested and active when they see themselves as competent (Barnett et al., 2008a,b; Stodden et al., 2009; Stuart et al., 2005).

High school physical education teachers can foster skill competency by establishing an instructional climate centered on mastery (Garn, Ware, et al., 2011; Hamilton & White, 2008; Ntoumanis et al., 2004). That type of climate focuses on self-improvement, provides students with choices, and de-emphasizes competition and peer comparisons.

By adolescence, students increasingly are aware of their interests and abilities, and they begin to select activities that fit those perceptions (Gallahue et al., 2012). While skillful students might enjoy a competitive-sport-based curriculum, most less-skilled students do not, instead preferring noncompetitive and cooperative activities (Garn, Cothran, et al., 2011). Student interest also is shaped by gender, with girls indicating a preference for fitness activities, dance and noncompetitive activities and dissatisfaction with a more traditional sport curriculum (Bryan et al., 2013; Couturier et al., 2007; Hannon & Ratcliffe, 2005; O'Neill et al., 2011; Ruiz et al., 2010; Wilkinson & Bretzing, 2011).

As seen in Standard 1, the high school outcomes are designed to address the needs

of all students by focusing on personal choice in lifetime activities, fitness activities and dance. The absence of competitive team sports found in invasion games and fielding/striking games is intentional. Invasion games are not considered lifelong physical activities and they do not meet the needs and interests of a large segment of high school students. Fielding/striking games also have been excluded because of the competitive team sport aspect as well as the limited amount of moderate to vigorous physical activity for most of the students on the field. Standard 2 outcomes have been designed to provide cognitive challenge for high school students by introducing basic concepts and principles from the subdisciplines of the profession. Cognitive challenge is essential for fostering student engagement and supports the goals of the Common Core State Standards.

While all the outcomes are important, there is a special emphasis on Standards 3 and 4 for the high school level. The knowledge and skills that are part of Standard 3 are essential for leading a physically active lifestyle in adulthood. The high school outcomes are centered on providing students with the opportunity to develop and implement personal physical activity plans under the guidance of the teacher. The teacher's feedback and support will ensure that students are capable of designing and using these types of plans independently once they graduate. Furthermore, the Standard 4 outcomes support the knowledge and skills of Standard 3 by promoting the development and refinement of life skills such as self-management, problem solving and communication. Those life skills are critical as students enter adulthood and must become self-directed in the decision to sustain physical activity in their lives. Finally, the outcomes of the first four standards provide the underpinning for Standard 5, in which students recognize the value of physical activity and make it a part of their lives.

Guidance for Using High School Outcomes

The high school outcomes are organized differently than the middle and elementary school outcomes in that they are divided into

two levels rather than individual grades. This structure allows for the wide variation in class time found in the United States as well as number of semesters or years required in high school physical education programs. **Level 1 outcomes** reflect the minimum knowledge and skills that students must acquire to be college or career ready at graduation. **Level 2 outcomes** allow students to build on Level 1 competencies by augmenting knowledge and skills considered desirable for college or career readiness.

For both Levels 1 and 2 outcomes, teachers must ensure sufficient practice time for skill acquisition. At the high school level, unit length should be extended to twice that of middle school, or about 15 to 16 classes for most units. With an extended unit length, students will be able to establish competency in the content and, subsequently, will be more likely to continue with the activity. In addition, extended units are more closely aligned with the way adults participate in physical activity, whether by engaging regularly on their own in an activity of interest or by enrolling in classes or recreation leagues.

In addition to increased unit length, block scheduling can be quite helpful in increasing the number of practice opportunities for student learning. The block schedule format allows ample time for changing clothes, providing instruction and engaging in practice tasks and small-sided or modified games. If students are engaged in a unit on some type of fitness activity, such as cardio–kick or spinning, it might not be realistic to keep them moving at moderate to vigorous intensity for the whole block period. But teachers can take advantage of the extra time in the block to integrate instruction on technique and fitness concepts while spending significant time engaged in the fitness activity itself.

In addition, the learning experiences of students can be enhanced in physical education class, as well as extended beyond the school day, through the use of **technology**. Supplemental information on physical activities, video clips, community resources and fitness- or wellness-tracking tools are all easily accessible online and from a variety of device applications. Both teachers and students can use those tools in creative ways to further learning. Find pointers on using technology to teach the standards and outcomes in chapter 9, which also contains supplemental resources available through SHAPE America.

Outcomes for High School (Grades 9-12)

By the end of high school, the learner will be college or career ready as demonstrated by the ability to plan and implement different types of personal fitness programs; demonstrate competency in two or more lifetime activities; describe key concepts associated with successful participation in physical activity; model responsible behavior while engaged in physical activity; and engage in physical activities that meet the need for self-expression, challenge, social interaction and enjoyment.

Table 5.1 provides the outcomes for the high school level. High school outcomes have been organized into two levels. Level 1 indicates the minimum knowledge and skills that students must attain to be college- or career-ready. Level 2 allows students to build on Level 1 competencies by augmenting knowledge and skills considered desirable for college or career readiness. Swimming skills and water-safety activities should be taught if facilities permit.

Table 5.1 High School Outcomes (Grades 9-12)

Standard 1. Demonstrates competency in a variety of motor skills and movement patterns.

Standard 1	Level 1	Level 2
Lifetime activities		
S1.H1	Demonstrates competency and/or refines activity-specific movement skills in 2 or more lifetime activities (outdoor pursuits, individual-performance activities, aquatics, net/wall games or target games).[i] (S1.H1.L1)	Refines activity-specific movement skills in 1 or more lifetime activities (outdoor pursuits, individual-performance activities, aquatics, net/wall games or target games).[ii] (S1.H1.L2)
Dance & rhythms		
S1.H2	Demonstrates competency in dance forms used in cultural and social occasions (e.g., weddings, parties), *or* demonstrates competency in 1 form of dance (e.g., ballet, modern, hip hop, tap). (S1.H2.L1)	Demonstrates competency in a form of dance by choreographing a dance or by giving a performance. (S1.H2.L2)
Fitness activities		
S1.H3	Demonstrates competency in 1 or more specialized skills in health-related fitness activities. (S1.H3.L1)	Demonstrates competency in 2 or more specialized skills in health-related fitness activities. (S1.H3.L2)

Standard 2. Applies knowledge of concepts, principles, strategies and tactics related to movement and performance.

Standard 2	Level 1	Level 2
Movement concepts, principles & knowledge		
S2.H1	Applies the terminology associated with exercise and participation in selected individual-performance activities, dance, net/wall games, target games, aquatics and/or outdoor pursuits appropriately. (S2.H1.L1)	Identifies and discusses the historical and cultural roles of games, sports and dance in a society.[iii] (S2.H1.L2)
S2.H2	Uses movement concepts and principles (e.g., force, motion, rotation) to analyze and improve performance of self and/or others in a selected skill.[iv] (S2.H2.L1)	Describes the speed/accuracy trade-off in throwing and striking skills.[v] (S2.H2.L2)
S2.H3	Creates a practice plan to improve performance for a self-selected skill. (S2.H3.L1)	Identifies the stages of learning a motor skill. (S2.H3.L2)
S2.H4	Identifies examples of social and technical dance forms. (S2.H4.L1)	Compares similarities and differences in various dance forms. (S2.H4.L2)

Standard 3. Demonstrates the knowledge and skills to achieve a health-enhancing level of physical activity and fitness.

Standard 3	Level 1	Level 2
Physical activity knowledge		
S3.H1	Discusses the benefits of a physically active lifestyle as it relates to college or career productivity. (S3.H1.L1)	Investigates the relationships among physical activity, nutrition, and body composition. (S3.H1.L2)
S3.H2	Evaluates the validity of claims made by commercial products and programs pertaining to fitness and a healthy, active lifestyle.[vi] (S3.H2.L1)	Analyzes and applies technology and social media as tools for supporting a healthy, active lifestyle.[vii] (S3.H2.L2)
S3.H3	Identifies issues associated with exercising in heat, humidity, and cold.[viii] (S3.H3.L1)	Applies rates of perceived exertion and pacing.[ix] (S3.H3.L2)
S3.H4	Evaluates—according to their benefits, social support network, and participation requirements—activities that can be pursued in the local environment.[x] (S3.H4.L1)	*If the outcome was not achieved in Level 1, it should be a focus in Level 2.*
S3.H5	Evaluates risks and safety factors that might affect physical activity preferences throughout the life cycle.[xi] (S3.H5.L1)	Analyzes the impact of life choices, economics, motivation, and accessibility on exercise adherence and participation in physical activity in college or career settings. (S3.H5.L2)
Engages in physical activity		
S3.H6	Participates several times a week in a self-selected lifetime activity, dance or fitness activity outside of the school day. (S3.H6.L1)	Creates a plan, trains for and participates in a community event with a focus on physical activity (e.g., 5K, triathlon, tournament, dance performance, cycling event).[xii] (S3.H6.L2)
Fitness knowledge		
S3.H7	Demonstrates appropriate technique in resistance-training machines and free weights.[xiii] (S3.H7.L1)	Designs and implements a strength and conditioning program that develops balance in opposing muscle groups (agonist–antagonist) and supports a healthy, active lifestyle.[xiv] (S3.H7.L2)
S3.H8	Relates physiological responses to individual levels of fitness and nutritional balance.[xv] (S3.H8.L1)	Identifies the different energy systems used in a selected physical activity (e.g., adenosine triphosphate and phosphocreatine, anaerobic glycolysis, aerobic).[xvi] (S3.H8.L2)
S3.H9	Identifies types of strength exercises (isometric, concentric, eccentric) and stretching exercises (static, proprioceptive neuromuscular facilitation (PNF), dynamic) for personal fitness development (e.g., strength, endurance, range of motion).[xvii] (S3.H9.L1)	Identifies the structure of skeletal muscle and fiber types as they relate to muscle development.[xviii] (S2.H9.L2)
S3.H10	Calculates target heart rate and applies that information to personal fitness plan. (S3.H10.L1)	Adjusts pacing to keep heart rate in the target zone, using available technology (e.g., pedometer, heart rate monitor), to self-monitor aerobic intensity. (S3.H10.L2)[xix]
Assessment & program planning		
S3.H11	Creates and implements a behavior-modificiation plan that enhances a healthy, active lifestyle in college or career settings. (S3.H11.L1)	Develops and maintains a fitness portfolio (e.g., assessment scores, goals for improvement, plan of activities for improvement, log of activities being done to reach goals, timeline for improvement).[xx] (S3.H11.L2)
S3.H12	Designs a fitness program, including all components of health-related fitness, for a college student and an employee in the learner's chosen field of work. (S3.H12.L1)	Analyzes the components of skill-related fitness in relation to life and career goals and designs an appropriate fitness program for those goals.[xxi] (S3.H12.L2)
Nutrition		
S3.H13	Designs and implements a nutrition plan to maintain an appropriate energy balance for a healthy, active lifestyle. (S3.H13.L1)	Creates a snack plan for before, during, and after exercise that addresses nutrition needs for each phase. (S3.H13.L2)
Stress management		
S3.H14	Identifies stress-management strategies (e.g., mental imagery, relaxation techniques, deep breathing, aerobic exercise, meditation) to reduce stress.[xxii] (S3.H14.L1)	Applies stress-management strategies (e.g., mental imagery, relaxation techniques, deep breathing, aerobic exercise, meditation) to reduce stress.[xxiii] (S3.H14.L2)

Standard 4. Exhibits responsible personal and social behavior that respects self and others.

Standard 4	Level 1	Level 2
Personal responsibility		
S4.H1	Employs effective self-management skills to analyze barriers and modify physical activity patterns appropriately as needed. [xxiv] (S4.H1.L1)	Accepts differences between personal characteristics and the idealized body images and elite performance levels portrayed in various media. [xxv] (S4.H1.L2)
Rules & etiquette		
S4.H2	Exhibits proper etiquette, respect for others and teamwork while engaging in physical activity and/or social dance. (S4.H2.L1)	Examines moral and ethical conduct in specific competitive situations (e.g., intentional fouls, performance-enhancing substances, gambling, current events in sport). [xxvi] (S4.H2.L2)
Working with others		
S4.H3	Uses communication skills and strategies that promote team or group dynamics. [xxvii] (S4.H3.L1)	Assumes a leadership role (e.g., task or group leader, referee, coach) in a physical activity setting. (S4.H3.L2)
S4.H4	Solves problems and thinks critically in physical activity or dance settings, both as an individual and in groups. (S4.H4.L1)	Accepts others' ideas, cultural diversity, and body types by engaging in cooperative and collaborative movement projects. (S4.H4.L2)
Safety		
S4.H5	Applies best practices for participating safely in physical activity, exercise and dance (e.g., injury prevention, proper alignment, hydration, use of equipment, implementation of rules, sun protection). (S4.H5.L1)	*If the outcome was not achieved in Level 1, it should be a focus in Level 2.*

Standard 5. Recognizes the value of physical activity for health, enjoyment, challenge, self-expression and/or social interaction.

Standard 5	Level 1	Level 2
Health		
S5.H1	Analyzes the health benefits of a self-selected physical activity. (S5.H1.L1)	*If the outcome was not achieved in Level 1, it should be a focus in Level 2.*
Challenge		
S5.H2	*Challenge is a focus in Level 2.*	Chooses an appropriate level of challenge to experience success and desire to participate in a self-selected physical activity.[xxviii] (S5.H2.L2)
Self-expression & enjoyment		
S5.H3	Selects and participates in physical activities or dance that meet the need for self-expression and enjoyment. (S5.H3.L1)	Identifies the uniqueness of creative dance as a means of self-expression. (S5.H3.L2)
Social interaction		
S5.H4	Identifies the opportunity for social support in a self-selected physical activity or dance. (S5.H4.L1)	Evaluates the opportunity for social interaction and social support in a self-selected physical activity or dance.[xxix] (S5.H4.L2)

[i]Manitoba Education and Training, School Programs Division, 2000, www.edu.gov.mb.ca/k12/cur/physhlth/grade_10.html?print.

[ii]Ibid.

[iii]NASPE, 1992, p. 15.

[iv]Ibid.

[v]Mohnsen, 2010).

[vi]NASPE, 1992, p. 16.

[vii]NASPE, 2012, p. 20.

[viii]Ibid., p. 9.

[ix]Ibid., p. 5.

[x]NASPE, 1992, p. 15.

[xi]Ibid.

[xii]NASPE, 2012, p. 27.

[xiii]Ibid., p. 6.

[xiv]Manitoba Education and Training, School Programs Division, 2000, www.edu.gov.mb.ca/k12/cur/physhlth/grade_9.html?print.

[xv]NASPE, 2012, p. 15.

[xvi]Ibid., p. 16.

[xvii]Manitoba Education and Training, School Programs Division, 2000, www.edu.gov.mb.ca/k12/cur/physhlth/grade_9.html?print.

[xviii]Ibid.

[xix]NASPE, 2012, p. 23.

[xx]*(Ohio) Physical Education Standards.* (p. 113).

[xxi]Superintendent of Public Instruction, Washington, 2008, p. 101.

[xxii]Manitoba Education and Training, School Programs Division, 2000, www.edu.gov.mb.ca/k12/cur/physhlth/grade_10.html?print.

[xxiii]Ibid.

[xxiv]NASPE, 2012, p. 25.

[xxv]NASPE, 1992, p. 16.

[xxvi]Manitoba Education and Training, School Programs Division, 2000, www.edu.gov.mb.ca/k12/cur/physhlth/grade_10.html?print.

[xxvii]Ibid.

[xxviii]*(Ohio) Physical Education Standards.* (p. 115).

[xxix]Ibid.

Operational Definitions of Activity Categories

- **Outdoor pursuits:** The outdoor environment is an important factor in student engagement in the activity. Activities might include but are not limited to recreational boating (e.g., kayaking, canoeing, sailing, rowing); hiking; backpacking; fishing; orienteering or geocaching; ice skating; skateboarding; snow or water skiing; snowboarding; snowshoeing; surfing; bouldering, traversing or climbing; mountain biking; adventure activities; and ropes courses. Selection of activities depends on the environmental opportunities within the geographical region.

- **Fitness activities:** Activities with a focus on improving or maintaining fitness. Fitness activities might include but are not limited to yoga, Pilates, resistance training, spinning, running, fitness walking, fitness swimming, kickboxing, cardio–kick, Zumba and exergaming.

- **Dance and rhythmic activities:** Activities that focus on dance or rhythms. Dance and rhythmic activities might include but are not limited to dance forms such as creative movement or dance, ballet, modern, ethnic or folk, hip hop, Latin, line, ballroom, social and square.

- **Aquatics:** Might include but are not limited to swimming, diving, synchronized swimming and water polo.

- **Individual-performance activities:** Might include but are not limited to gymnastics, figure skating, track and field, multisport events, in-line skating, wrestling, self-defense and skateboarding.

- **Games and sports:** Includes the games categories of invasion, net/wall, target and fielding/striking.

- **Lifetime activities:** Includes the categories of outdoor pursuits, selected individual-performance activities, aquatics and net/wall and target games. *Note:* Invasion and fielding/striking games have been excluded from the high school outcomes because these activities require team participation and are less suited to lifelong participation.

Section II

Implementing the Outcomes

Chapter 6

Outcomes Skills and Knowledge Across Grade Levels

Table 6.1 serves as a quick reference for practitioners when planning and implementing lessons leading to student attainment of the grade-level outcomes. The chart specifies the knowledge and skills expected at each grade level and illustrates how learning progresses across those grade levels. The arrows indicate the grade levels in which the knowledge and skills should be a focus of instruction; shaded cells indicate the grade levels in which the knowledge and skills need not be a focus of instruction. Skills and knowledge are coded for introduction and practice (emerging), demonstration of critical elements (maturing) and application in different contexts (applying).

The following terms are used throughout the table:

E = **Emerging.** Students participate in deliberate practice tasks that will lead to skill and knowledge acquisition.

M = **Maturing.** Students can demonstrate the critical elements of the motor skills and knowledge components of the grade-level outcomes, which will continue to be refined with practice.

A = **Applying.** Students can demonstrate the critical elements of the motor skills and knowledge components of the grade-level outcomes in a variety of physical activity environments.

Table 6.1 Scope & Sequence for K-12 Physical Education

Standard 1. Motor skills & movement patterns

	Kindergarten	Grade 1	Grade 2	Grade 3	Grade 4	Grade 5	Grade 6	Grade 7	Grade 8	High School
Hopping	E	M	A	→						→
Galloping	E	M	A	→						→
Running	E	→	M	A	→					→
Sliding	E	M	A	→						→
Skipping	E	→	M	A	→					→
Leaping		E	→	M	A	→				→
Jumping & landing	E	→	→	M	A	→				→
• Spring & step					E	M	A	→		→
• Jump stop							E	M	A	→
• Jump rope	E	→	→	M	A	→	i	i	i	i
Balance	E	→	→	M	→	A	→			→
Weight transfer			E	M	→		A	→		→
Rolling	E	→	→	→	→	M	A	→		→
Curling & stretching	E	→	M	→	→	A	→			→
Twisting & bending		E	M	→	→	A	→			→
Throwing										
• Underhand	E	→	M	→	→	→	A	→		→
• Overhand	E	→	→	→	→	M	A	→		→
Catching	E	→	→	→	M	A	→			→
Dribbling/ball control										
• Hands	E	→	→	→	M	A	→			→
• Feet		E	→	→	→	M	A	→		→
• With implement				E	→	M	A	→		→
Kicking	E	→	→	→	M	→	A	→		→
Volleying										
• Underhand	E	→	→	→	M	A	→			→
• Overhead					E	→	ii	ii	ii	ii
• Set								E	→	M
Striking—with short implement	E	→	→	→	M	A	→			→
• Fore/backhand							E	→	M	A
Striking—with long implement			E	→	→	M	A	→		→
• Fore/backhand								E	→	M
Combining locomotors & manipulatives					E	→	M	→	A	→
Combining jumping, landing, locomotors & manipulatives						E	M	A	→	→
Combining balance & weight transfers			E	→	→	→	M	→	A	→

iJump rope becomes a fitness activity after grade 5 and is absorbed into Standard 3. Engages in fitness activities.

iiOverhead volley becomes a specialized skill for volleyball—setting—that begins being taught in middle school.

	Kindergarten	Grade 1	Grade 2	Grade 3	Grade 4	Grade 5	Grade 6	Grade 7	Grade 8	High School
Serving										
• Underhand							E	M	A	→
• Overhand							E	→	→	M
Shooting on goal						E	→	→	M	*
Passing & receiving										
• Hands						E	→	M	→	*
• Feet				E	→		→	→	M	*
• With implement							E	→	M	*
• Forearm pass							E	→	M	A
• Lead pass						E	→	M	→	*
• Give & go							E	M	→	*
Offensive skills										
• Pivots							E	M	A	*
• Fakes							E	→	M	*
• Jab step							E	→	M	*
• Screen									E	*
Defensive skills										
• Drop step							E	→	M	*
• Defensive or athletic stance							E	→	M	*

*Teaching team sports skills is not recommended at the high school level. See chapter 5 for rationale.

Standard 2. Concepts & strategies

	Kindergarten	Grade 1	Grade 2	Grade 3	Grade 4	Grade 5	Grade 6	Grade 7	Grade 8	High School
Movement concepts, principles & knowledge	E	→			M	→	A	→		→
Strategies & tactics				E	→		M	→	A	→
Communication (games)							E	→	M	A
Creating space (invasion)										
• Varying pathways, speed, direction							E	M	A	*
• Varying type of pass							E	M	A	*
• Selecting appropriate offensive tactics with object							E	→	M	*
• Selecting appropriate offensive tactics without object							E	→	M	*
• Using width & length of the field/court							E	→	M	*
• Playing with one player up (e.g., 2v1)							E	→	M	*
Reducing space (invasion)										
• Changing size & shape of the defender's body							E	M	A	*
• Changing angle to gain competitive advantage							E	→	M	*
• Denying the pass/player progress							E	→		*
• Playing with one player down (e.g., 1v2)							E	→		*
Transition (invasion)							E	M	A	*
Creating space (net/wall)										
• Varying force, angle and/or direction to gain competitive advantage							E	→	M	A
• Using offensive tactic/shot to move opponent out of position							E	→		M
Reducing space (net/wall)										
• Returning to home position							E	→	M	A
• Shifting to reduce angle for return							E	→		M
Target										
• Selecting appropriate shot/club							E	→	M	A
• Applying blocking strategy							E	→		M
• Varying speed & trajectory							E	→	M	A
Fielding/striking										
• Applying offensive strategies								E	→	*
• Reducing open spaces							E	→	M	*

*Teaching team sports skills is not recommended at the high school level. See chapter 5 for rationale.

Standard 3. Health-enhancing level of fitness & physical activity

	Kindergarten	Grade 1	Grade 2	Grade 3	Grade 4	Grade 5	Grade 6	Grade 7	Grade 8	High School
Physical activity knowledge	E				→	M		→	A	→
Engages in physical activity	E				→	M			→	A
Fitness knowledge	E				→	M			→	A
Assessment & program planning				E	→	M			→ A	→
Nutrition	E						→	M		→ A
Stress management							E		→	M

Standard 4. Responsible personal & social behavior

	Kindergarten	Grade 1	Grade 2	Grade 3	Grade 4	Grade 5	Grade 6	Grade 7	Grade 8	High School
Demonstrating personal responsibility	E		→	M		→	A			→
Accepting feedback	E		→	M		→	A			→
Working with others	E		→	M		→	A			→
Following rules & etiquette			E		→	M	→	A		→
Safety	E	→	M		→	A				→

Standard 5. Recognizes the value of physical activity

	Kindergarten	Grade 1	Grade 2	Grade 3	Grade 4	Grade 5	Grade 6	Grade 7	Grade 8	High School
For health			E			→	M		→	A
For challenge			E			→	M		→	A
For self-expression/enjoyment	E				→	M			→	A
For social interaction				E		→	M		→	A

Chapter 7

Teaching for Content and Skill Mastery

Essential to meeting the National Standards and Grade-Level Outcomes for K-12 Physical Education is the careful creation of learning experiences (deliberate practice tasks) that ensure that K-12 students have the opportunity to demonstrate content and skill mastery. The challenge for practitioners is creating effective learning experiences and practice tasks that engage students in learning. This chapter focuses on the creation of effective learning experiences (deliberate practice tasks) as part of the learning cycle. Guidelines provide teachers with the tools needed to design learning experiences based on the unique characteristics of their students, content and teaching environment.

Defining Deliberate Practice

Ericsson, Krampe, and Tesch-Romer (1993) defined deliberate practice as learning experiences with the primary purposes of "attaining and improving skills." Attaining and improving skills mandates structured practice tasks designed to correct weaknesses and improve performance. Deliberate practice is characterized by students' active engagement (cognitively and physically) in learning experiences that require concentration and effort. Often, learners engage in drills that have no effect on skill acquisition or learning because the drill does not require their active engagement in the practice task. Drills that are not challenging or do not require problem solving have little effect on student learning. Here is an example: A middle school teacher has taught three different passes used in the invasion game of basketball. In parallel lines, students pass to a stationary classmate using the three passes. While drilling students on correct technique, the task fails to challenge or engage them cognitively. To challenge and engage students, the teacher could place students in a grid, have them use the three passes to a moving partner and select the most appropriate pass based on their partner's movement. The task now challenges and cognitively engages students since they must select the most effective pass based on the partner's movement. The second learning experience is more deliberate and more closely resembles game conditions.

While Ericsson (2006) identified 10,000 hours or 10 years as the benchmark for attaining an expert level, he also posited that it could take as little as 50 hours of training and experience to attain an acceptable level of performance. If physical educators can plan sequential deliberate practice learning experiences, their students can reach acceptable levels of performance for grade-level outcomes in 50 hours or less of practice and instruction. For students to reach competency, teachers will need to plan and implement deliberate practice tasks that address performance and knowledge weaknesses. The focus must be on long-term achievement of grade-level outcomes. That will require teachers to think beyond one unit of instruction and to focus on the long-term goal of skill and knowledge competency. Most students cannot achieve a mature overhand throwing pattern through a three-week unit of instruction on throwing. They will need to be engaged in focused, deliberate practice tasks over multiple classes and years.

Creating deliberate practice tasks is a key to developing movement competency essential for meeting the goal of a lifetime of physical activity for all students. Researchers (e.g., Barnett et al., 2008 a, b; Castelli & Valley, 2007; Ennis, 2011; Kambas et al., 2012; Portman, 2003; Stodden, et al., 2008, 2009) have associated perceived competency as a key variable in a lifetime of physical activity. Teachers are charged with developing learning experiences that increase skill to ensure that students have the

Deliberate Practice

The concept of deliberate practice grew out of the research by Ericsson (1996, 2001, 2002, 2003a, b, 2004, 2006) and colleagues (e.g., Ericsson et al., 1993; Ericsson & Lehman, 1996) on obtaining elite performance levels. Researchers on expert performance encompassed various disciplines from music (e.g., Gruson, 1988; Krampe & Ericsson, 1996; Sloboda, Davidson, Howe, & Moore, 1996) to chess (e.g., Charness, 1981; Simon & Chase, 1973) to athletics (e.g., Schulz & Curnow, 1988; Strakes, Deakin, Allard, Hodges, & Hayes, 1996). The following commonalities were found across all disciplines.

1. Achievement of expert performance occurs only after multiple years of experience, beginning in childhood. The most commonly cited rule is 10 years and 10,000 hours of practice (Ericsson, 2006).

2. Simply playing or having experience does not lead to expert performance. Practice must be deliberate, systematic and designed to address performance errors or weaknesses.

3. Improvement is dependent on the effort extended by learners and learner engagement. Learners taking part in drills or games that do not involve decision making or cognitive engagement do not improve.

4. Feedback provided by a qualified coach or teacher is essential for improvement. The role of the teacher or coach is to design practice tasks that address performance errors and provide specific corrective feedback.

5. Deliberate practice requires concentration by the learner. Because concentration is required, practice tasks should be focused and of short duration.

movement competency to be lifetime movers. That is accomplished through deliberate and focused practice tasks and teacher-designed learning experiences that challenge and engage students in the learning process.

Deliberate Practice Tasks

Teachers are charged with developing learning experiences that lead to student attainment of lesson objectives, unit goals and state and national standards. What follows are five guidelines based on concepts taken from motor learning and control research for designing deliberate practice tasks linked specifically to attaining identified objectives and goals. Each teaching environment is unique and provides a different set of challenges. These guidelines will allow teachers to develop learning experiences specific to their environment and account for individual differences within classes.

Guideline 1. Practice tasks must be deliberate.

If the focus of the lesson is on dribbling in self-space, then all practice tasks must focus on the skill. As younger children master dribbling in self-space by dribbling 5 times, then 10, then 15, the teacher begins to manipulate the environmental demands of the task but the focus remains on dribbling. Task variations of dribbling in self-space could include challenges such as changing the height or speed of the dribble, but the key component of the task would be controlled dribbling in self-space. Once students achieve control of the ball, the teacher would begin to manipulate the environment to include dribbling in general space by varying speed and direction. The initial self-space dribbling tasks would be of short duration because the practice tasks do not reflect the context in which the skill is used.

Guideline 2. Practice within the context of the skill.

Teachers should mirror the context in which the skill is used when creating practice tasks. For example, if passing and **receiving** on the move are required, the practice task should mirror those essential elements. Having a stationary student pass to a stationary receiver provides little to no learning on passing and receiving on the move. Learning how to pass or receive on the move mandates practicing the task while moving. Teachers must design a series of practice tasks that allow students to increase the complexity of the environment incrementally. For example, practice might begin by having the passer stationary and the receiver moving. Next, both the passer and receiver are moving. Adding a defender provides another layer of

Dribbling Task

Grade 2

Often, teachers move to modified game play before learners have mastered the skills necessary for success. For example, a second-grade teacher introduces the skill of dribbling, has the class practice for minutes and then moves immediately into a modified game that requires learners to dribble, travel and pass to teammates. Most learners won't be successful because they still are struggling with dribbling, even without the added complexity of traveling and passing to teammates. Some learners will struggle with traveling and dribbling, others will have difficulty with simply dribbling five times consecutively, while others with experience outside of class might be able to combine dribbling with traveling. Deliberate practice requires sequential and progressive increases in environmental complexity based on performers' skill levels.

Moving too quickly into a more complex environment required for game play violates Ericsson's (1996) research on expert performance and deliberate practice. Researchers (e.g., Ericsson et al., 1993; Ericsson & Lehman, 1996) have found that game play does not automatically lead to skill acquisition or improved performance. To ensure that learning occurs, learners need extended practice time with tasks that are progressively more challenging, based on individual performance levels (differentiated instruction) and focused on specific performance criteria.

complexity, which then can be modified by constraining the actions of the defender (e.g., block passes but do not take the ball from the passer). The teacher maintains the essential elements of the context of the skill by manipulating the performance environment. If learners are struggling with catching and receiving while moving, the teacher could use a slower-moving object or slow the pace of the practice task but should not change the essential context of the skill.

Guideline 3. Practice tasks must be challenging.

Teachers must design practice tasks that are physically and mentally challenging to students. That requires the manipulation of environmental constraints such as equipment, number of individuals involved in the task, size of space, with or without defense, number of response options, etc., to ensure student engagement of both higher-skilled and lower-skilled learners. Teachers know the developmental and skill levels of their students and should use that information to design differentiated practice tasks to ensure that all students engage in the learning experience. Providing choices to students based on skill levels within practice tasks is essential for differentiation of instruction.

Students should have input on entry points, equipment, size of the space, conditions such as stationary or moving and with or without defense, as well as other environmental constraints based on their skill level. Those choices begin early in elementary school with decisions such as size and type of ball, space needed and travel or no travel for the practice task. As learners mature, decisions on type of activities, partner or group or practice or modified game play are appropriate.

One way to ensure that tasks are challenging and require cognitive engagement is to use exploration and problem solving as teaching approaches. At the elementary level, learners need opportunities to discover the many ways they can create movements and move; explore movement concepts related to space, time, effort and relationships; and demonstrate problem solving through movement. Later, middle and high school students can discover the science that underpins efficient movement, apply knowledge of the physiology of health-related fitness to create personal fitness plans and use behavioral theory to develop behavior-modifications plans.

Guideline 4. All students should engage in the practice task.

The number of opportunities that students have to use and apply knowledge and skill correlates directly with learning and student engagement. Researchers (e.g., Silverman, Tyson, & Morford, 1988; Solmon & Lee, 1996; van der Mars, 2006) have found that the amount of appropriate practice has a significant effect on student learning. The challenge to teachers is creating appropriate practice tasks that encompass the varying skill levels within a class. Tasks that are challenging for low-level performers will not be challenging for high-level performers, and tasks that are challenging for high-level performers soon will frustrate low-level performers. Here are some suggestions for maximizing student engagement.

- **Ability grouping.** Placing learners in groups with similar skills and knowledge allows teachers to use the same practice task in the class. Higher-level perform- ers will challenge each other by increasing the speed and/or complexity of their responses while lower-performing students will have opportunities to challenge each other at the appropriate skill level. Placing higher-performing learners with lower-performing learners to increase learning for both is a misconception and has little support in the research literature. Higher-performing learners will dominate

CREATING OPEN SPACE
GRADE 5

The objective for the learning task is for students to practice creating open space using the give and go and lead pass for the invasion game of basketball. Students pair up in a grid (a square or rectangular space of varying sizes marked by cones). Students choose the equipment to be used (basketball, volleyball trainer or foam ball) and size of grid. Students select partners or are grouped by ability. The lesson would include three practice tasks in a sequence of increasing complexity, with students working with their partners in the grid without defense. Each practice task lasts 45 seconds to 1 minute before the teacher modifies the task to increase or decrease complexity based on student responses.

The practice tasks that follow are of short duration to ensure that students stay engaged, make decisions, think about their movements and gain multiple practice opportunities. Specifying the actual time length for each task will help maintain student motivation and activity levels.

Practice Task 1

Students receive a pass and move to another position within the grid (give and go). Students are instructed to create a straight pathway in a diagonal line to a corner of the grid on the "go" part of the movement. The stationary passer throws a lead pass to where the partner is moving within the grid. It's important for the passer to anticipate the speed of the partner and to throw to where the partner is going (not to where the partner is). The passer concentrates on throwing to a point in front of the receiver. As soon as the pass is made, the passer moves to another position in the grid. The receiver now becomes the passer and must anticipate where the partner is moving and throw to that point within the grid.

Practice Task 2

After one sequence, the teacher can modify the task to increase or decrease complexity. Students who are struggling might be asked to move directly to a cone in a straight line and not on a diagonal. If throwing a lead pass is the performance error, students could practice passing to a cone as the partner moves across the grid. Students who are successful then could be asked to vary the type of pass to the partner and to increase the speed of the diagonal motion. Students in each grid would decide on the next step based on their performance. The teacher provides the options based on each pair's performance level.

Practice Task 3

Students increase or decrease the grid size so that receivers have more or fewer options and passers must anticipate movement over a greater or smaller distance. After each practice task, students must debrief and reflect on their performance. They must discuss how to improve their performance and what changes they need to make for them to be more effective.

the practice task or modified game and lower-performing students soon become disinterested bystanders.

- **Differentiated instruction.** The teacher provides different practice options to allow for varying performance levels within the class. For example, some learners in a badminton class might opt for a "shorty" racket or a larger shuttlecock to adapt a practice task. Higher-skilled performers could opt for a regulation racket and shuttlecock. Giving learners choices on various entry points or equipment for a practice task allows for differences in skill levels. At the elementary level, learners could explore striking a balloon using noodles, short or long lollipop paddles or their hands. Giving learners choices allows them to control and take responsibility for their learning. Mosston and Ashworth (2002) refer to this as the "slanty rope" approach, in which learners select the entry point that works for them (choosing to jump over the lower or higher end of the "slanty rope"). The teacher's role is to ensure that learners are making suitable

Task Card

Passing and Receiving

At your station, your group can select one of the following tasks to practice passing and receiving while moving. You need to base your selection on the group's current skill level, with the intent of improving and challenging your current skill level. Remember to focus on the following two components of the task.

- Passers are stationary. Make sure that you lead your receiver with your pass. Throw to where the receiver is moving to and not where the receiver is. Remember that your passes should be crisp and accurate.
- Receivers must indicate where they would like to receive the pass by providing the throwers with a target. All receivers must be moving when they catch the pass but must stop within one step of making the catch. Concentrate on reaching for the pass and giving with the ball. Receivers immediately become passers.

Task 1 Parameters

Select either a yarn or a foam ball for this practice task. Concentrate on throwing to a cone located in the corner as your partner takes a straight or diagonal pathway to the cone. Remember to anticipate when your partner will arrive at the cone. Receivers will concentrate on providing a target, reaching for the ball, continuing to move and stopping within one step of making the catch.

Task 2 Parameters

Select either a playground ball or volleyball trainer for this practice task. Concentrate on throwing a crisp and accurate pass to where the receiver is moving within the grid. Receivers will use change of direction or pathway to move away from the passer. Receivers will concentrate on providing a target, changing direction or pathways, reaching for the ball and stopping within one step of making the catch.

Task 3 Parameters

Select either a basketball or disc for this practice task. Concentrate on throwing a crisp and accurate pass to a moving receiver. Anticipate where and when the receiver will be open to receive the pass. The passer should use a different pass each time he or she throws. Receivers will change direction, speed or pathway to become open for the pass reception. Receivers should concentrate on providing a target for the passer; changing direction, pathway or speed; reaching for the ball or disc; and stopping within one step of making the catch.

choices and moving beyond their current skill levels.

A second way of differentiating instruction is to vary practice tasks within the group. Creating stations with varying challenges or modifying activities allows for individual differences. Place task cards in grids or stations to define the parameters of the practice task, based on skill level. A task card would identify three options with varying challenge levels, and learners select the appropriate option based on skill level.

- **Teaching by invitation.** As learners engage in whole-group, individual or small-group practice, teachers can invite individual learners or groups of learners to increase or decrease the complexity of the task (Graham, Holt/Hale, & Parker, 2013). These invitations allow teachers to differentiate instruction based on performance on the practice task.

Guideline 5. Teach for transfer of learning.

Conceptual knowledge and movement principles should be taught as concepts applied to multiple movements and fitness activities. If students understand and apply concepts, they become self-directed learners using conceptual knowledge to problem solve and improve movement skills and fitness levels. A good example found in the National Standards & Grade-Level Outcomes for K-12 Physical Education involves the use of game categories. Tactics and strategies used in invasion, net/target and field/striking games are taught as concepts that apply to all games in the category. A "give and go" is an offensive tactic used in invasion games to create open space. Students need to understand how open space is created through skills such as give and go, pivot and fakes, and apply those skills to all invasion games. Rules, skills, space and equipment can vary from game to game, but the tactics remain the same for creating open space.

For the transfer of conceptual knowledge to occur, teachers must teach for transfer by point-

ing out common elements across various games, sports and fitness. If teachers are working on offensive strategies and skills that create open space for invasion games, they need practice tasks that allow students to apply the concept and use the skill in varying environments. Teachers can design the lesson so that students practice the concept while rotating through **grids** stocked with different equipment. In one grid, students practice a give and go by kicking a soccer ball, while in another grid, students pass and catch a disc. Students spend two minutes in each grid and begin to understand that the give and go is used in invasion sports to create open space.

By designing deliberate practice tasks that require students to apply concepts in various environmental contexts, teachers ensure that transfer of learning occurs. At the end of five rotations, students should discuss the practice tasks and talk about the common elements they discovered. They could be asked to create a list of other common skills and tactics used in invasion games. Partnering conceptual-knowledge practice with skill practice ensures cognitive engagement, increases the movement challenge and facilitates transfer of learning.

Designing practice tasks that allow students to use and discover movement principles is another method of ensuring transfer. Students need to know the how and why of movement. Teachers can develop sequences of deliberate practice tasks that allow students to explore movements and discover fundamental principles of movement efficiency. The overhand throwing pattern provides an example. Students start by lying on the floor and attempting to throw to partners using an overhand motion. The teacher can ask such questions as "How is your movement restricted?" or "Why did you find it difficult to throw with power or for distance?" Next, students then move to their knees and throw with the overhand motion to their partners. Students now compare and contrast the two tasks and identify what changed in the second tasks that allowed more power production. In the third task, students stand and throw without a forward step. The fourth task would have them using a unilateral step, and the final task would have them sideways to the target with a bilateral step. Students would debrief after each task and list advantages and disadvantages for each. By the end of the practice task sequence, students

will discover the role of angular rotation in producing power for the overhand throw. With teacher reinforcement, students will be able to apply the concept in other activities.

Transfer of knowledge and skill does not occur accidentally or automatically as part of game play or as the result of the teacher lecturing. Transfer of knowledge and concepts must be planned, and students must have opportunities to practice and apply the concepts. While students may know components of the **FITT** (frequency, intensity, time and type) formula, they also need to transfer the components of the formula to various activities. Can they apply the formula to weight training and a walking program? Having students apply the formula to a single activity will limit their ability to transfer the knowledge to multiple contexts. Because the goal for physical education is a physically literate individual, it's important that students have multiple opportunities to apply concepts and principles. Eventually, students will become self-directed learners as they prepare for college and careers. It's important that they exit their years of physical education with the tools (knowledge of movement and fitness concepts) for making informed decisions on fitness and physical activity, creating and implementing personal activity plans and becoming movers for a lifetime.

EXPLORATION EXPERIENCE FOR BALANCE AND STABILITY

Purpose

Explore various concepts related to balance and stability. Students will manipulate their base of support, location of their center of gravity and location of their line of gravity to determine the effect on balance and stability. At the end of the experience, students will determine how these changes affect their movements.

Key Points for Balance

1. Balance is defined as the maintenance of equilibrium while stationary (static) or moving (dynamic).
2. Center of gravity
   - An imaginary point about which weight is equally distributed or balanced.
   - Can be raised or lowered to increase or decrease stability.
   - Can fall inside or outside of the base of support.
   - Moves in the direction of additional weight.

- Generally located in pelvic region for adults.
- Relatively higher in children and relatively lower in women.
- Position varies with body proportions and posture assumed.
- The closer center of gravity is to the center of the base of support, the greater the stability.

3. Line of gravity
  - Imaginary line that extends through the center of gravity straight down to center of the earth.
  - If the line of gravity is outside the base of support, there is less stability.

4. Base of support
  - A wide base of support provides more stability.
  - A narrow base of support provides less stability.
  - To maintain a stable position, individuals must exert force in the opposite direction to an oncoming force (opposition increases stability).
  - The nearer the line of gravity is to the middle of the base of support, the greater the stability.
  - Ready positions in sport are based on the ability of an individual to move quickly in any direction. That requires a higher center of gravity and a narrower base of support.

Activity for Balance and Stability

Partner Push-Off (center of gravity, line of gravity, and base of support)

1. Partners face each other and stand within an arm's length with palms pressed against each other's palms.
2. Keeping palms pressed against each other's palms, students attempt to knock their partners off balance.
3. Students attempt the task four times. Each time they vary their foot position:
   - Feet together
   - Feet shoulder-width apart
   - Feet staggered front and back
   - Standing on tiptoes

At the end of the four attempts, students answer the following questions:

1. What was the most stable position? Justify your answer.
2. What was the least stable position? Justify your answer.
3. Based on this experience, what would be the most stable position for the human body? Justify your answer.

The Role of Feedback and Deliberate Practice

Feedback in tandem with deliberate practice will speed skill and knowledge acquisition and increase retention. Ericsson et al. (1993) stated, "In the absence of adequate feedback, efficient learning is impossible and improvement only minimal even for highly motivated subjects" (p. 367). Two types of feedback related to the process or the product of the skill are knowledge of results and knowledge of performance.

Knowledge of results provides learners with feedback specific to the degree of success of the movement as it relates to the target task. That type of product feedback includes information such as "How close did I come to hitting the bull's-eye on the target?" or "Did I make the basket?" Knowledge of results is provided as a result of the movement, and learners can see the results.

Teachers can provide corrective feedback to students by designing practice tasks that address specific weaknesses and provide knowledge of results. The handstand in gymnastics provides an example. Placing the hands outside the width of the shoulders is a common performance error. If students place their hands directly under the shoulders (bone on top of bone), it becomes a balance task and not a strength move. No matter how many times a teacher tells students that their arms are outside their shoulders, students don't feel and can't see the correction. One strategy is for students to put chalk on their hands and then attempt a handstand, which creates handprints on the mat. If the teacher instructs students to then place their feet where the handprints are, they soon discover that their hands are outside the width of their shoulders. The practice task itself provides feedback on the performance error of the hand position. Students then can continue to practice the handstand and receive vital information on correct hand position through completing the practice tasks.

Knowledge of performance provides learners with corrective feedback on the pattern or technique of the movement. This type of process feedback takes the form of teacher comments such as "Nice job on stepping in opposition" or "Your ball went out of bounds because your racket face was too open." Knowledge of performance is augmented feedback that is provided either by a peer or a teacher and is specific to the quality of the movement pattern.

Providing Feedback

Providing enough one-on-one feedback in large classes is difficult. Fortunately, all feedback doesn't have to come from teachers; it can come from a variety of sources and includes group-specific feedback, continuous assessment, peer assessment and self-assessment.

- **Group-specific feedback.** Deliberate practice provides teachers with multiple opportunities for group-specific feedback. Because practice tasks are focused and limited in scope, teachers constantly are refining or extending tasks based on learner performance. Between each refinement or extension, teachers provide feedback on performance that is specific to the practice task. Deliberate practice sequences gradually refine performance based on feedback and repetition (Ericsson, 2006). Because every class will have multiple practice tasks, teachers have multiple opportunities to provide specific, corrective feedback.

- **Continuous assessment.** Continuous assessment is a vital part of the learning cycle and provides specific corrective feedback to students. By assessing students, teachers discover transition points at which to increase or decrease task complexity. Ongoing assessment also provides students with specific feedback on their progress and identifies areas of strength and weakness. The assessment data indicate weaknesses to address in the next deliberate practice tasks as well as strengths to reinforce. Many teachers use "instant activities" for the first two minutes or so of the class. This is an opportunity for teachers to make a quick assessment of the skill or concept taught in the previous lesson. While students practice, the teacher assesses the critical elements and determines whether more practice time is needed.

Overhand Throwing Practice

A study completed by Capio, Poolton, Sit, Eguia & Master (2013) found that starting with a large target and reducing the size of the target slowly over time resulted in improved overhand throwing motion and performance for students with intellectual disabilities. The progression allowed learners to reduce the number of initial errors and to begin to make self-corrections before the size of the target was reduced slightly for the next practice task. This is using an errorless motor-learning approach (Maxwell, Masters, Kerr & Weedon, 2001).

The teacher manipulates the environment to reduce the number of initial errors so that students make a limited number of self-corrections at each level based on performance results. The outcome of the performance provides feedback at each level, which the learner uses to make changes.

The study documented that both process and outcome improved over time. The researchers wrote, "Our findings indicate that reduced errors in the initial stages of learning better facilitate the development of an object control skill" (p. 303).

- **Peer assessment.** Peer assessment can supplement teacher feedback and enhance learning for all students. Student observers can demonstrate and increase their understanding by providing focused feedback to classmates. Observers become active participants if they, too, have a learning experience linked to the practice task. For the Creating Open Space practice task on p. 75, observers could be charged with counting the number of completed passes, providing qualitative feedback on passing technique or drawing each of the pathways made by the individuals in the grid. For peers to provide meaningful feedback, teachers must provide them with checklists, rubrics or guidelines on what to look for during the practice task. At the end of a one-minute task, observers provide written or oral feedback to their classmates on the number of completed passes, quality of their passing technique or the pathways used. This form of peer assessment provides specific corrective or outcome-based feedback to learners while engaging observers in the learning task. A combination of peer and teacher assessment bridges the feedback gap created by too many students and too little time in physical education.

- **Self-assessment.** With the growing use of technology, learners have more opportunities for self-assessment. iPads and other devices allow learners to film their performance at a station or learning center and view it immediately. Learners also can use pedometers, accelerometers or heart rate monitors to assess their activity levels during class. Fitness and physical activity data can be charted so that students can follow their progress over time. The teacher's role is to provide the necessary guidelines for students to appropriately complete self-assessments and become self-directed learners.

Maximizing the Number of Practice Opportunities

The number of opportunities for students to use or apply skill and knowledge correlates directly with learning. Engaging in learning experiences outside students' current levels of proficiency provides them with challenge and motivation. Teachers need to design practice tasks that maximize practice opportunities while extending movement challenges for individual learners within their proximal zones of development. Here are four guidelines for maximizing practice opportunities and extending movement challenges.

Guideline 1. Ensure adequate equipment and space.

Every student should have access to adequate equipment and space. Time spent waiting to use shared equipment or for space to become available is lost instructional time. An alternative to having students wait to share space or equipment is using nonregulation equipment for practice tasks. Elementary school students can learn to dribble with playground balls, and middle school students can substitute playground balls for dribbling practice if not enough basketballs are available. Use sponge balls or volleyball trainers when practicing

Group-Specific Feedback

Group-specific feedback occurs when the teacher stops the class to identify a performance error that the majority of students are making and provides specific feedback on how to correct the common performance error. For example, if students are practicing a backhand in pickleball from a partner soft toss and most students are contacting the ball too late in the swing with their weight on the back foot, the teacher would have all students in the class focus on contacting the ball in front of the lead foot and concentrate on shifting their weight forward as they swing through the ball. The teacher could combine group-specific feedback with a modification to the task. Students might extend the task backward by practicing from a self-toss and not a soft toss from a partner. That simplifies the performance environment and allows students to concentrate on just one performance error.

forearm passes. If equipment is limited, use station work as an alternative to waiting for equipment or space to become available. Learners not engaged in the main practice tasks can take part in self-directed learning tasks in stations or by using task cards.

Guideline 2. Work in small groups.

All learning experiences should involve enough equipment for the entire group or small subgroups of no more than four learners. Reducing the number of students in a group ensures more touches for each group member. Deliberate practice mandates that learning experiences actively engage learners in the task. Full-sided or large-group learning experiences in which the "real game" is played (soccer with one ball and 22 players; basketball with one ball and 10 players) reduce the number of practice opportunities and fail to engage all learners. In large-group activities, higher-skilled players dominate, which limits opportunities for lower-skilled players.

Guideline 3. Limit the amount and type of competition in class.

Research (e.g., Bernstein et al., 2011; Bevans et al., 2010; Garn, Cothran, et al., 2011; Garn, Ware, et al., 2011) supports that competitive full-sided game play does not maximize learning opportunities for all students. The evidence is clear that higher-performing students dominate game play, with lower-performing students having fewer opportunities for active participation (Bernstein et al., 2011; Garn, Cothran, et al., 2011). In addition, many learners are turned off by competition. Competition pits students against each other and encourages performance comparison. Deliberate practice tasks encourage learners to compare previous performance levels with current levels. Success is measured in terms of improved performance and mastery.

Another method of lessening the negative effect of competition is focusing on small-sided play that maximizes participation and minimizes bystanders (Bevans et al., 2012). Engaging students in small-sided games lessens the opportunities for social and skill comparison.

Guideline 4: Score modified games and practice tasks based on the use of the skill.

Teachers can score modified games based on the use of the skill in the context of the game or practice task. Students playing 2v2 modi-

fied volleyball can score only if their team uses three hits to return the ball to the other side. This will require students to focus on three hits as a strategy and it rewards teams that actually use the strategy. If a team returns the ball to its opponent's side in fewer than three hits, play continues but the opponent team does not score a point on the return. Rewarding students for using new skills and strategies through creative score keeping increases the likelihood that meaningful practice will continue. Even if the outcome is not optimal, students are rewarded for attempting the skill. If the focus is on the outcome (i.e., scoring a point), students are not likely to focus on skill development.

Practice Schedules, Constant Practice and Varied Practice

Teachers often mass practice tasks. If the unit is on throwing, teachers will have students move through a sequence of throwing activities for the majority of the class period. This is a block or massed practice schedule. On face value, it might seem like the most efficient way to practice because students are provided with multiple practice opportunities in one class period. What seems intrinsically true, though,

is not supported by researchers. Schmidt and Wrisberg (2008) noted that massing practice tends to raise practice performance but depress learning and retention. While massing practice gives students a short-term practice gain, it actually interferes with the long-term goal of knowledge and skill competency. The lack of long-term performance gains is due largely to a lack of contextual interference effect in massed, block or constant practice tasks.

Contextual interference effect occurs anytime a performer switches from one activity to another. The simple act of switching to a new, unrelated or related task cognitively re-engages the student, which can lead to increased learning. The new task requires the learner to problem solve, focus attention and increase effort simply because it is a new and different challenge. An improved practice sequence for the overhand throw is to plan three or four deliberate practice tasks interspersed throughout the class period. Learners might begin with a sequence of three practice tasks on throwing at the beginning of the class period. They then move to other skills or tactics before performing another set of deliberate throwing-practice tasks in the middle of class. Next, learners switch to deliberate practice application tasks and finish the class period with another sequence of overhand throwing

Competition Volleyball

Competitive volleyball provides an example of how full-sided games can reduce opportunities for students to improve skills. In many physical education classes, students will engage in 6v6, 8v8 or even 12v12 volleyball games. Experience shows that few students will receive opportunities to contact the ball. Higher-skilled students will jump in front of lower-skilled students or lower-skilled students will get out of the way for fear of embarrassment or public failure. No one wants to lose a point for the team!

One alternative to full-sided games is small-sided games (2v2 or 3v3) on badminton courts, coupled with grouping students by ability level. Ability grouping in small-sided games allows for higher-skilled players to challenge one another while lower-skilled players are equally challenged

at their own performance level.

Reducing the number of students on the court allows students more opportunities to engage in the task (i.e., more touches on the ball). If space is an issue, some students can play in small-sided games while other students work in stations on specific skills. Game play is alternated with skill practice. Having all students standing out on a 12v12 volleyball game doesn't foster student engagement, increase physical activity time or lead to skill acquisition or learning.

Having students compete against their personal best is a type of competition that can motivate and engage students. Their opponent is not a peer but rather their personal best. This requires students to focus on improving performance and helps establish a mastery environment.

practice. This is an example of random or varied practice, in which learners practice a variety of skills and apply various concepts throughout the class periods, which creates high levels of contextual interference effect.

Researchers in motor learning (e.g., Schmidt & Bjork, 1992; Shea & Morgan, 1979) have confirmed that high levels of contextual interference effect enhance learning and retention. Students must practice retrieving the schema of movement for a given task, executing it, processing feedback and storing the information for future attempts as the task. If practice involves a block of repetitions of the same task, there is no need for (or practice of) retrieval and storage of the information.

Creating practice tasks with high levels of contextual interference effect is essential for games and sports in which learners must adapt to an ever-changing environment. Invasion, net/wall and fielding/striking games all require performers to use what are considered open skills: those in which the performer's response is dependent on varying factors such as the opponent's position or the speed and location of the shot. They must respond or anticipate changes in the environment on every shot,

pass or hit. For learners to achieve competency in these activities, their practice tasks must mirror this dynamic performance context.

Gentile (1972) has identified two stages for both open and **closed skills (stable, non-dynamic environment)**. Stage 1 for both is achieving success in an initial practice environment and developing a general motor schema. This stage is relatively short in duration. Stage 2 for a closed skill is refinement of the motor schema and developing consistency of the pattern in a stable, nondynamic (closed) environment. For an open skill, Stage 2 learners begin to get the idea of the movement pattern that will be successful. In tennis, that would involve practicing the swing without contacting an object, hitting into the fence from a well-placed soft toss or returning balls from a ball machine. That allows learners to have an "Aha!" experience, thinking "Now I get the idea."

The next stage in Gentile's (1972) model for open skills is diversification. Because the essential context requires learners to respond to an ever-changing environment, practice tasks must be designed to allow learners to systematically practice varying conditions. At this stage, diversification of the spatial and tempo-

Driving Range and a Bucket of Balls

Practicing a golf swing by hitting a bucket of balls is common with most recreational golfers. The golfer hits a quantity of balls using the same club to groove the swing or correct some performance error. Many times the golfer indeed will demonstrate improvement after hitting the entire bucket of balls, but on the golf course the next day the corrections seem to have disappeared.

Hitting a bucket of balls using one or two clubs is an example of a massed practice condition that leads to improvement during practice but that doesn't transfer to the actual activity. While playing golf, players are confronted with a different and unique set of environmental contexts each time they hit a shot. The ball might be in the rough, on a hill or in a divot. All those and other environmental contexts require golfers to problem-solve based on their evaluation of the current goal of the movement. More important, they get one attempt (okay, maybe one mulligan)

and not multiple swings.

One way in which golfers could build practice variability into their driving-range practice is to hit a different club on each stroke (more game-like) or limit the multiple swings to fewer than 10 per club. They could take a score card and pretend they are on the course. Let's say hole 1 is a par 4 of 310 yards. The golfer chooses a driver and takes five swings with the driver from the tee. The best tee shot travels 180 yards, so now, the ball is 130 yards from the green. The golfer decides to play a 7 iron and hit five swings from the ground with the goal of 130 yards to place the ball on the green.

This is a more variable practice schedule and will lead to more long-term learning. For each shot the golfer must problem solve (which club for which distance) and determine what is needed. The practice is more game-like and engages the learner in the task.

ral variables of the schema must be practiced. Too much practice with a ball machine will improve performance on returning balls from a ball machine but will not lead to long-term competency in tennis. Teachers need to create practice task sequences in which students learn to anticipate where and when the ball is going to land and how to adjust the swing based on those variables. These essential elements in tennis can be learned only through practice tasks that mirror the context of the game or sport. That requires learners to participate in multiple and varying deliberate practice tasks in one class period. Such a variable practice schedule will lead to increased learning and retention.

Massed, constant or block practice can be useful during the initial stage of learning an open skill or for skills in which the environment remains stable (closed skills). In closed skills, performers have more control over their execution of the skill because they are not responding directly to an opponent. While a forehand or backhand in tennis is executed in response to the opponent's hit (open), the serve is controlled by the server (closed). Teeing off in golf or shooting a foul shot in basketball are other examples of a nondynamic (closed) environment for skill execution. Closed skills require learners to duplicate the same movement with consistency in a stable environment. Learners must have enough repetitions to develop a movement schema, which often is best accomplished in a block practice schedule. Many closed skills used in target games benefit from a block or constant practice schedule, as well. Dart throwing is an example of a target game that requires duplication of a consistent movement in a stable environment. Learners practice the task using a standardized dart board from a standardized distance. Because the environment is stable, consistency of movement is the goal. Closed-skill performance benefits from a more constant and blocked practice schedule.

Teachers decide what type of deliberate practice schedule is appropriate based on the learner, the task and the context of the skill. The role of the teacher is to create deliberate practice task sequences that lead to students' learning based on all environmental factors. Pulling a tried-and-true drill from the Internet or a book will not allow for the uniqueness of students or differing skill levels. The teacher is the expert, and students need teachers to use that expertise to plan appropriate practice tasks.

Striking

Striking is the last of the fundamental motor skills to mature. It also is a coincidence-anticipation skill, which requires learners to predict or to anticipate where and when the swing will intersect with the moving object. Coincidence-anticipation skills such as catching and striking are most influenced by practice. Students have to learn to anticipate where the moving object is going and decide on what is the optimal point to intersect with the object. This ability to anticipate and make appropriate spatial decisions is improved through practice.

Students need lots of opportunities to practice making these predictions and developing the timing to intercept the object at the optimal point. This is in addition to developing an appropriate swing, grip and footwork to ensure power and control.

The difficulty with planning practice tasks for striking is having two beginners attempting to practice or rally with each other. Because neither player can hit with any control or consistency, keeping a rally going is impossible. Alternatives include soft-toss practice, in which students strike the ball into the tennis fence from a soft toss; having students hit to a partner from a dropped ball using a "shorty" racket to ensure more control and consistency as the partner attempts to return the ball; using a ball machine; or striking against a rebounding wall. Until players can return balls consistently in those contexts, they should not attempt a rally with a partner.

The most important component of a striking practice task is the number of opportunities to make contact with a moving object. That requires teachers to have lots of balls available for practice, as the majority of time should be spent on striking and not retrieving the one or two balls provided for practice.

Deliberate practice tasks require students to be cognitively engaged and to concentrate. That mandates practice tasks of short duration (no more than two minutes) that require learners to problem-solve or think about the movement and reflect the essential context of the skill. Lengthening a practice task to four minutes doesn't double the learning. Once a practice task extends to four or five minutes, students lose concentration and cognitive engagement is lost. Students simply go through the motions and don't increase their skill competency.

A more effective approach is to limit the amount of initial instruction to one or two critical elements. Learners practice those elements for one to two minutes before the teacher determines whether the practice task needs to be extended or refined. When the teacher makes that determination, the student practices a refinement or extension for one to two minutes. Once learners show that they have the idea of the movement, the teacher adds another critical element and repeats a practice sequence. At any time during the instructional or practice sequence, students should have the choice of moving forward or repeating the former practice task. If students have not mastered the prerequisite practice task, they will just find failure at the next level. It's important to give students the opportunity to practice skills at their developmental levels.

Students bring a unique set of movement experiences and are at various skill levels in each class. They should be allowed to opt for the next practice task or opt to repeat the former task. The teacher's role is to plan appropriate deliberate practice sequences and guide student choices.

Creating a Mastery Climate

Creating deliberate practice tasks that facilitate skill and knowledge acquisition and retention leads to a mastery climate in the classroom. In a mastery-climate classroom, students define success as achieving through hard work and personal improvement (Bevans et al., 2010; Garn, Cothran, et al., 2011; Garn, Ware, et al., 2011; Ommundsen, 2006). They view mistakes as part of the learning process. Students identify feelings of satisfaction and

competency when developing new skills or knowledge, which is intrinsic to a mastery climate. The expectation of students and teachers is attainment of personal goals and objectives. A mastery climate ensures that students have opportunities to participate in multiple learning experiences without evaluative judgments or comparisons with peers. Learning becomes about achieving the objective or mastering the content through sequential and progressive learning experiences.

Multiple researchers (Chen & Darst, 2001; Garn, Cothran, et al., 2011; Garn, Ware, et al., 2011; Hamilton & White, 2008; Smith & St. Pierre, 2009; Treasure & Roberts, 2001; Zhang et al., 2011) identify the creation of a mastery climate as essential for student motivation and learning in physical education. Students need to enter the classroom expecting to work hard to improve, to accept mistakes as part of the process and to engage in a series of well-designed practice tasks leading to content mastery.

Summary

High-quality instruction times deliberate practice equals skill and knowledge acquisition (high-quality instruction × deliberate practice = skill and knowledge acquisition). Researchers (e.g., Ericsson, 1996; Ericsson & Lehman, 1996) report that deliberate practice multiplies the effect of high-quality instruction and increases time on task during class. Because learning experiences are of short duration, focus on one or two critical elements and involve individual or small groups, the time and opportunities for practicing and applying concepts and knowledge increases. The increased time in deliberate and focused practice leads to increased learning and skill acquisition.

The importance of developing physically literate individuals must not be underestimated. Perceived competency is a key variable in predicting a lifetime of physical activity (e.g., Barnett et al., 2008 a, b; Castelli & Valley, 2007; Ennis, 2011; Kambas et al., 2012; Portman, 2003; Stodden et al., 2008, 2009), and students must leave K-12 physical education as competent movers. To attain that goal, teachers must plan and implement progressive and sequential learning experiences that challenge and engage students in the learning process. Establishing a mastery climate in which all students expect to work hard, participate without evaluative judgment and gain competence will affect students' physical activity levels positively both in and out of class. High-quality instruction coupled with deliberate practice leads to physically literate individuals who will be active for a lifetime.

Chapter 8

Evidence of Student Learning

At the beginning of the 21st century, federal, state and local governments began to increase accountability measures for K-12 schools across all disciplines. This movement adopted principles of standards-based reforms, with the expectation that all students will demonstrate academic excellence. This continued movement toward standards-based reform also is reflected in the Common Core State Standards movement that dates from 2010. Inherent in standards-based reform is the development of clear, measurable standards for all students (NASPE, 2010) which are reflected in the current National Standards &Grade-Level Outcomes for K-12 Physical Education.

Linked to standards-based learning is standards-based accountability. Standards-based accountability mandates ongoing assessment of students' progress, which requires teachers to systematically assess, collect data on and provide evidence of student growth (i.e., that students are meeting grade-level outcomes). The best way to measure students' progress is to use **criterion-referenced performance standards** (grade-level outcomes), which replace **norm-referenced** rankings, or comparisons with other students (NASPE, 2010).

This chapter begins with guidelines for developing assessments for physical education, with samples of the various types of assessments. These guidelines will allow teachers to create assessments aligned with grade-level outcomes. Because teachers cannot assess all of the outcomes at each grade level, this chapter also provides guidance on selecting grade-level outcomes for assessment.

Assessment in physical education comes with a unique set of challenges. Often, elementary physical education teachers will interact with 600 students in a week, and middle and high school physical educators see almost as many. That makes collecting, analyzing and tracking assessment data a demanding and daunting challenge. To help practitioners integrate meaningful assessment, the second part of this chapter provides tips on assessing and tracking large groups of students.

No matter the challenges, standards-based learning requires continuing assessment. Advances in software and technology have made assessing, collecting data on and tracking students' progress easier and more doable than ever before. Physical educators no longer can rely on observation as their primary assessment method or measure students' progress simply by participation. Standards-based reform, coupled with increased accountability, mandates a change in how physical educators assess student progress and account for meeting the National Standards.

The Goal of Assessment

Assessment is the gathering of evidence about student achievement and making inferences on student progress based on the evidence. That requires teachers to collect and track assessment data over time. Data analysis guides instructional decision making as well as planning deliberate practice tasks, determining next steps and evaluating the attainment of objectives or outcomes. Students are the central focus in deciding types and timing of assessments. Grades provide little specific feedback to students; therefore, a quality assessment plan includes different types of assessments that provide meaningful feedback to students on their progress. Aggregated class-assessment data provide evidence of teacher and program effectiveness that teachers can share with parents and administrators.

Assessment is continuous and occurs throughout the learning sequence. Preassessments—including formal pretests, teacher

observations and/or review of assessment data from the previous year—allow teachers to formulate a picture of where students are at the beginning of a learning sequence or unit. Formative assessments that are ongoing during instruction—including checks for understanding, exit slips, worksheets and quizzes—allow teachers to track student progress, adapt instruction and place students in instructional groups.

Summative assessments—including written tests, skills tests, fitness plans, activity logs and other end-of-instruction evaluations—occur at the close of a unit or instructional sequence. These assessments allow teachers to determine students' levels of achievement at the end of the unit and provide a comprehensive summary of each student's progress. Summative assess-

ments identify both strengths and weaknesses and provide guidance on how students can improve performance. By comparing formative assessment data with summative assessment data, teachers determine the effect of the instructional sequence on student learning. Over time, summative assessment data provide concrete evidence of whether students have achieved grade-level outcomes, allow teachers to reflect on instructional effectiveness and provide evidence about program success.

All types of assessments—including traditional summative assessments and other forms such as checklists, rating scales and rubrics—are appropriate in physical education because they provide evidence of student learning. So long as the selected assessment links directly to the intent of the outcome, produces meaningful data and provides feedback to students, it is appropriate.

Guidelines for Developing Assessments

All quality assessment tools provide guidelines for evaluating performance, align with the assignment or instructional objective and designate performance criteria (process and/or product). But they vary in the specificity that they provide to learners regarding performance. When selecting or creating an assessment tool, teachers should consider the complexity of criterion behaviors, the practicality of using the tool and the degree of specificity desired. What follows is some guidance on creating checklists and developing rating scales and rubrics.

Checklists identify whether individual performance criteria are present or absent. A checklist is a simple "Yes" or "No" assessment tool that does not measure how well the criteria are met (quality). Checklists are useful with, but not limited to, outcomes that have one skill or knowledge component. For example, the grade 3 outcome S1.E16.3 states, "Catches a gently tossed hand-size ball from a partner, demonstrating four of the five critical elements of a mature pattern." Teachers could assess that outcome with a checklist. First, the teacher would identify criterion behaviors (critical elements for a mature catching pattern; see p. 22). The next step involves developing descriptors using parallel language structure, which requires teachers to avoid using a short descriptive phrase for one criterion behavior and a long descriptive sentence for another criterion behavior. The length and structure of the descriptors remain consistent for all criterion behaviors on the checklist. Finally, a simple "Yes" (criterion is present) or "No" (criterion is absent) evaluates student performance. See figure 8.1 for a sample checklist.

Teachers can combine checklists with other assessment tools. Developing a simple "Yes/No" checklist listing the parts of a middle school-level fitness plan (goals, warm-up and cool-down, nutrition log, workout plan with FITT formula and activity data) provides feedback to students on completeness of the assignment. Teachers would use a checklist to identify which parts of the assignment are missing, then use a different assessment tool to determine the quality of the assignment's elements.

Assignment Versus Assessment

Assessments differ from assignments. An assignment for the grade 8 outcome S3.M18.8 ("Designs and implements a program to improve levels of health-related fitness and nutrition") might include developing and implementing a fitness plan. The fitness plan assignment might include setting goals based on fitness assessment data (S3.M15.8), developing workouts with a warm-up/cool-down regimen (S3.M12.8), using a nutrition log to record eating habits, using the FITT formula to create an **overload** for the described workout plan (S3.M11.8) and reporting data on activity levels using a pedometer or other technology (S3.M8.8).

Teachers create assessments that evaluate each of the required elements in the assignment. These tools address and align specifically with each component in the assignment. Assessment tools appropriate for this assignment might include a checklist, rating scale and/or rubric.

Checklists are simple to design, easy to use, effective in providing feedback and useful as peer assessments. They also are suitable for a variety of skills, such as a high clear in badminton, a backhand in tennis or dribbling in soccer. Creating a spreadsheet using Excel or Google forms allows teachers to track checklist data over time and determine student achievement of outcomes across grade levels.

A **rating scale** is similar to a checklist, with added information on the extent to which criterion behavior is met. This is accomplished by a gradation of criteria across levels. Most rating scales identify at least three and no more than five levels. As the number of levels increases on a rating scale, the distinction between levels decreases and the agreement among scorers increases. Some rating scales differentiate among levels based on the frequency at which the criterion behavior occurs (e.g., 25 percent, 50 percent or 75 percent of the time; seldom, sometimes or consistently). Other rating scales define criterion behavior holistically, with descriptions at each level. Teachers should use rating scales that use parallel

structure for the descriptors and that have clear distinctions among levels. Evaluators must be able to differentiate among behaviors based on the rating scale.

Rating scales provide information on how often or to what extent learners are demon-

Grade 3 Catching (S3.E16.3) Checklist

Name:_____

Circle Y or N to indicate which of the criterion behaviors are present or absent.

Watches the ball all the way into the hands	Y	N
Extends arms outward to reach for the ball	Y	N
Thumbs in for catch above the waist	Y	N
Thumbs out for catch at or below the waist	Y	N
Catches with hands only	Y	N
Pulls the ball into body while making the catch	Y	N

Figure 8.1 Sample checklist.

strating criterion behaviors. To be effective, individual items on the rating scale should be easily observable and scored independently. When using frequency to differentiate among levels, the percentage of occurrence must be defined. For example, a frequency level could be defined as 1 = never demonstrates the criterion, 2 = less than 50 percent of the time, 3 = 50 percent of the time but less than 75 percent, 4 = 75 percent of the time but less than 100 percent and 5 = always demonstrates the criterion. Based on how often the criterion behaviors occur, teachers make inferences on learners' levels of mastery of criterion behaviors. See figure 8.2 for a sample rating scale.

Holistic rating scales use paragraph descriptions to identify criterion behaviors at each level. A generic 1-to-4 or 1-to-5 scale, with 1 representing a low-level performance and 4 or 5 representing a high-level performance, can be used for each item. Levels are differentiated through the description of criterion behaviors at that level. That requires teachers to define and describe observable behaviors for each level. Judgment about the quality of the performance is based on *all* the criteria in the paragraph simultaneously. If any one criterion behavior is not demonstrated by learners, they should be scored at the next level below. See figure 8.3 for an example.

Another approach to creating a holistic rating scale is to list specific criterion behaviors at each of the levels. Learners must demonstrate *all* criterion behaviors in the level. Task-specific skills (e.g., forearm pass in volleyball, game-play strategies) often use holistic rating scales. Criterion behaviors differentiate among levels of competency and provide learners with specific feedback. The rating scale that follows provides learners with information on their current levels of proficiency based on the identified criterion behaviors. Teachers can

Dribbling Frequency Rating Scale

Outcome: Dribbles in general space with control of ball and body while increasing and decreasing speed. (S1.E17.4b)

Name:_____

Criteria, component or concepts	Level 1	Level 2	Level 3	Level 4	Level 5
Head and eyes up, with eyes looking over the ball					
Contact with finger pads and slightly behind the ball					
Ball to the side and in front of the body while moving in general space					
Control of ball and body while traveling and dribbling					
Avoids contact with others while traveling and dribbling in general space					

1 = Does not demonstrate criterion behavior

2 = Demonstrates criterion behavior less than 25 percent of the time

3 = Demonstrates criterion behavior more than 25 percent of the time but less than 50 percent

4 = Demonstrates criterion behavior more than 50 percent of the time but less than 75 percent

5 = Demonstrates criterion behavior more than 75 percent of the time but less than 100 percent

Figure 8.2 Sample rating scale.

use rating scales as a formative assessment (i.e., to determine grouping of students) or as a summative peer assessment. Using rating scales to determine the impact of instruction on students' learning requires teachers to analyze and compare pre-assessment and post-assessment data. See figure 8.4 as a sample.

Rubrics are assessment and instructional tools that identify criterion behaviors for at least two levels of performance. That allows teachers to match students' performances to well-defined criterion behaviors and delineates the degree to which the criterion is met. Each level of the rubric identifies and describes criterion behaviors that contain the essential elements of the task along with the range or continuum of performance expectations for learners. The format for a rubric usually is a grid or matrix that identifies scaled levels of performance based on identified criterion behaviors. Identified criterion behaviors at each level (strong, middle and weak levels of performance) are specific to assignments or learning tasks, aligned with performance objectives or outcomes and used to evaluate learners' performances based on the range or continuum of performance identified on the rubric.

Rubrics outline specific expectations for learners through descriptors of criterion behaviors for assignments or tasks. Descriptors at each level communicate expectations and define "what counts" at each level. By defining specific expectations at each level, learners begin to understand differences between weak and strong performance based on the content of the rubric. Using a rubric allows for more consistent evaluation of performance by teachers; makes teacher expectations clear; provides learners with specific, corrective and detailed feedback; and supports learning and skill development.

Holistic Rating Scale

Outcome: Cooperates with multiple classmates on problem-solving initiatives, including adventure activities, large-group initiatives and game play. (S4.M5.8)

Level 4: The student gave and listened to others' ideas during the activity and encouraged others with both verbal (e.g., "Nice job" or "Good idea") or nonverbal (e.g., high five or smile) communication. Provided suggestions on strategies for increasing group effectiveness that the group often accepted. The student demonstrated a willingness to try others' suggestions through both body language and verbal communication. The student demonstrated leadership by organizing others and accepting responsibility for various roles within the group.

Level 3: The student offered ideas and listened to others' ideas during the activity and encouraged others with both verbal (e.g., "Nice job" or "Good idea") or nonverbal (e.g., high five or smile) communication. The student provided suggestions on strategies for increasing group effectiveness that the group occasionally accepted. The student demonstrated a willingness to try others' suggestions through both body language and verbal communication. The student accepted responsibility for various roles within the group.

Level 2: The student listened to others' ideas during the activity and provided nonverbal encouragement (e.g., smile or high five) but provided little verbal encouragement. The student offered suggestions but cooperated only if the group accepted the suggestions. The student participated in all the activities but without enthusiasm and made minor contributions to the group's success. The student would take responsibility only for self-selected roles in the group.

Level 1: The student was distracted or failed to listen during group activity and provided no verbal or nonverbal encouragement to group members. The student never offered suggestions and seemed disinterested in contributing to the group. The student's participation in the activity was limited and often made it difficult for the group to succeed.

Figure 8.3 Sample holistic rating scale.

Developing quality rubrics requires teachers to create descriptors that include essential elements of tasks or assignments and that set performance expectations for each level. Descriptors describe precisely what the performance "looks like" at each level and how one level is different from the next. The more precise the description, the more clarity in the rubric. AAHPERD's *PE Metrics* (2010) series contains numerous examples of rubrics for K-12 physical education and provides a rich resource for developing descriptors. Other sources include the list of critical elements for fundamental motor skills in this book, textbooks, online resources, state curriculum documents (e.g., Ohio, South Carolina) and SHAPE America's Assessment Series of books (see chapter 9).

Rubrics come in two types: holistic and analytical. A holistic rubric assigns a level of performance based on multiple criteria and performance as a whole. That allows teachers to evaluate learners' performances quickly and affords an overview of learners' capabilities. Holistic rubrics allow teachers to more easily evaluate large groups of students and provide at least a formative assessment of performance levels. The advantage to using holistic rubrics, when compared with checklists, is the time saved in the evaluation process. An example of a holistic rubric appears in table 8.1.

Converting the checklist for grade 3 catching on p. 86 to a holistic rubric involves grouping performance criteria into levels. With a checklist, teachers must check off each individual critical element for each student, whereas using a holistic rubric allows teachers to assign a single number based on learners' overall performances. The checklist does provide both teachers and learners with more specific feedback on performance, while the holistic rubric gives an overall picture. The alignment of the assessment to the outcome decides the selection of the assessment.

While reviewing table 8.1, note that the lowest and highest performance levels are identified by what the evaluator would actually see. When developing descriptors for each level, teachers should avoid describing the lowest level as the absence of a criterion behavior or the highest level as more of the criterion behavior. The example does not simply state that "hands are not used exclusively for the catch" but rather describes the behavior likely to occur, which is "ball is trapped with the body or the hands are closed too early or too late." The lowest-level descriptors describe the behaviors likely to occur and not simply the absence of a behavior. The highest-level descriptors define the extension of the criterion behaviors. In the example below, students at the Applying level (3) make adjustments based on the ball's speed and trajectory and anticipate the catch. Both of those behaviors are extensions of criterion behaviors described in the Maturing level (2).

Rating Scale Criterion Behaviors for Net Game Competency, Tennis

Outcome: Demonstrates competency or refines activity-specific movement skills in two or more lifetime activities (outdoor pursuits, individual-performance activities, aquatics, net/wall games or target games). (S1.H1.L1)

Level 3: Moves to ball before it crosses the net; returns ball crosscourt or down the line, as appropriate, to gain a **competitive advantage**; recovers to baseline or moves to net as appropriate. Shot is hit with pace and accuracy.

Level 2: Moves to ball after it crosses the net; returns ball crosscourt; recovers to baseline. Shot is hit with moderate pace and accuracy.

Level 1: Waits for ball in stationary position; returns ball straight ahead; maintains court position with no recovery. Shot is hit with accuracy.

Figure 8.4 Sample rating scale criterion behaviors.

Table 8.1 Holistic Rubric, Grade 3 Catching (S1.E16.4)

Developing (1)	Maturing (2)	Applying (3)
Student loses sight of the ball or turns head in "fear" response. The ball is trapped with the body, or the hands close too late or too early. Hands do not adjust based on the flight of the ball. Ball often bounces off the hands because there is no "give" upon contact.	Student watches the ball all the way into the hands, with arms reaching out for the ball. Thumb placement (in or out) varies based on the location of the ball (above or below waist). Student uses only the hands for the catch, and pulls the ball into the body upon contact.	Student watches the ball into the hands with full extension of the arms. Student modifies hand positions based on the ball's speed and trajectory. Student uses only the hands to catch the ball thrown with varying trajectories and speeds. Student anticipates the catch and gives with the ball each time.

Holistic rubrics allow teachers to evaluate overall performance of a class quickly. The following example could serve as a preassessment to determine group assignments or to identify high or low performers before moving into instruction. Holistic rubrics are useful for assessing learners' readiness. A holistic striking rubric would allow teachers to discover starting points for instruction in grade 3 since a mature striking pattern is not an expectation until grade 5. Holistic rubrics provide teachers with a snapshot of learners' performance levels that aids instructional decision making, differentiation of instruction and the ability grouping of students.

Analytical rubrics divide assignments or tasks into independent component parts, with criterion behaviors defined for each part and across levels. Independent evaluation of each component allows for more extensive and specific feedback to students. Using an analytical rubric allows teachers to disaggregate multiple criteria into one scoring tool that facilitates assessment of complex performance or assignments with multiple components. Each component or trait of the performance or assignment is defined separately. Assessing performance occurs on a continuum defined by criterion behaviors unique to each component. Using an analytical rubric allows teachers to weight individual items. If one component or trait is more important than another, teachers can simply assign a multiplier to the more important component or trait. In the analytical rubric provided in table 8.2, grade 3 catching performance (S1.E16.4) is divided into component parts and evaluated separately. The analytical rubric provides more specific feedback to learners on each component of the catching skill and allows a more complete analysis.

Analytical rubrics often are used with more complex skills, performance concepts (e.g., game play) or assignments that assess multiple outcomes. One of the advantages of using analytical rubrics is the ability to assess more than one outcome with one rubric, which reduces time spent on assessment. Analytical rubrics also allow teachers to set performance expectations across components or traits while defining expectations to learners. All rubrics (holistic or analytical) should align with performance objectives and the description of the task or assignment and should be shared with learners.

The analytical rubric example in table 8.3 is specific to outcomes under Standards 1, 2 and 4 at the middle school level. The rubric, used during modified game play, assesses skills, strategies and knowledge of rules in an authentic environment. Authentic environments require students to complete tasks in real-world settings that mirror the context in which the skill or strategy would be used. While teachers can assess throwing in isolation (nonauthentic environment), they also can assess throwing during game play (authentic environment). Components for the analytical rubric for modified invasion-game play include the skills of throwing (S1.M5.7) and dribbling (S1.M8.7) as well as the strategies of give and go (S2.M2.7) and anticipating on defense (S2.M5.7). The rubric also helps assess knowledge of rules (S4.M6.7). Each component is evaluated separately and key components are weighted based on their relative importance. The value of each component equals the level achieved times the weight of the component.

Analytical rubrics provide opportunities for physical educators to address Common Core State Standards. At the high school level, students create and implement a behavior-change plan to address behavioral changes such as increasing physical activity levels (S3.H11.L1)

Table 8.2 Analytic Rubric, Grade 3 Catching (S1.E16.4)

Level of proficiency	Hand position	Body position	Anticipation & spatial adjustments	Catching various objects
Level 3 (Mature)	Uses only the hands to make the catch. Hand position is adjusted based on whether catch is made above or below waist. Object contacted with both hands with simultaneous closure of hands, which is well timed.	Gives with the ball at the shoulders and elbows in anticipation of the catch. Eyes remain on object, and no fear response is present with any change in speed of object.	Moves effectively in anticipation of the object's flight. Both feet and hands correctly anticipate the object's flight. Demonstrates effective catching while stationary and moving.	Effectively catches a variety of objects while moving and stationary. Caught objects include a tennis ball, a disc and a football.
Level 2 (Emerging)	Uses only the hands to make the catch. Hand placement is inconsistent with where the catch is made (above or below waist). Object contacted with both hands simultaneously with a well-timed closure of the hands.	Gives with the ball at the elbows in anticipation of the catch but is inconsistent with the give at the shoulders. Eyes remain on object, and no fear response is present if the ball is moving at a moderate speed.	Inconsistent movement in anticipation of the object's flight. Makes adjustments to the flight of the ball with only the hands and not the feet. Demonstrates effective catching while stationary.	Effectively catches round objects while stationary but has difficulty adjusting to other shapes or types of objects.
Level 1 (Developmental)	Often traps ball to the body and does not use only the hands to make the catch. Hand placement is inconsistent with object's flight, and closure of hands is ill timed.	Does not give with the object in anticipation of the catch. Eyes remain on the object, but a fear response is present.	Does not anticipate the object's flight and has difficulty catching while stationary. Does catch from a self-toss.	Does not consistently catch any object. Does catch slow-moving objects such as scarves or balloons.

Table 8.3 Modified Invasion Game-Play Rubric, Grade 7

Competency level	Throwing Weight = 1 (S1.M5.7)	Dribbling Weight = 1 (S1.M8.7)	Give and go Weight = 2 (S2.M2.7)	Anticipation Weight = 2 (S2.M5.7)	Knowledge of rules Weight = 1 (S4.M6.7)
Level 1	Throws, while stationary, a leading pass to a moving receiver but fails to anticipate the receiver's movements on the throw.	Dribbles with dominant hand only, with little change in direction or speed. Looks down at the ball often while dribbling.	Often stands still after passing the ball to a receiver. Must be reminded to move to a new space after passing, or hesitates before moving.	Defender faces guards opposing receiver and is unaware of the location of the passer, or defender guards the ball and is unaware of the location of the receiver.	Modified game play is disrupted due to disagreements over rules, or teacher is consulted repeatedly to clarify rules.
Level 2	Throws, while moving, a leading pass to a moving receiver, anticipating the receiver's speed and direction.	Dribbles with dominant and nondominant hands while changing speed and direction.	Moves immediately to a new space after passing the ball to a receiver. There is no hesitation upon release of the pass to move to a new space.	Defender anticipates the speed of the object or the defender to deflect the pass or disrupt the offense.	Modified game play is self-officiated, with few consultations with teacher on rules.
Level 3	Throws, while moving, a leading pass to a moving receiver with pace and accuracy.	Dribbles with control using dominant and nondominant hands while changing speed and direction. Uses the dribble effectively to create open space.	Recognizes and moves immediately to open space after passing the ball to a receiver.	Defender anticipates the speed of the object and the defender to deflect or intercept the pass.	Modified game play is self-officiated, with no consultation with teacher on rules. Students modify rules to increase the challenge.

or modifying nutritional intake (S3.H13.L1).

Meeting Outcome S3.H13.L1 lends itself to the inclusion of Common Core writing and math standards. Students could graph activity levels or nutritional-intake data each day for two weeks and determine what days they were most active or inactive or ingested the fewest or greatest number of calories. Using the graph and the analysis of baseline data, students would reflect on what precipitated lower or higher levels of activity or eating and identify specific behavioral triggers. Based on this analysis, students would set goals to change behaviors, design and implement a behavior-change plan, collect data from the plan as implemented and reflect on final results. Students would use written language and math skills related to analysis of data to design and implement the plan and reflect on final results.

Creating a behavior-change plan requires students to use discipline-specific language to describe each part of the plan, justify their choices based on an analysis of activity or nutritional-log data and apply critical-thinking and problem-solving skills. This comprehensive assignment allows for assessment of discipline-specific outcomes and Common Core State Standards. A sample format or outline for a behavior-change plan assignment and an analytical rubric for assessing the assignment is provided in figures 8.5 and 8.6. The categories include discipline-specific criterion behaviors along with math, writing and problem-solving criterion behaviors for Common Core State Standards.

Other Forms of Assessment

Checklists, rating scales and rubrics (holistic and analytic) are forms of criterion-referenced assessments that evaluate process. Other assessments are norm-referenced. The former President's Challenge Physical Fitness Test was a norm-referenced assessment in which a student's percentage score was determined by age- and gender-level norms. On this test, a fifth-grader compared the number of curl-ups he or she completed with the percentage level on the chart for that number. Norm-referenced assessments such as this allow teachers to compare their students with national norms based on age and gender.

Skills tests are another type of assessment that is used often in physical education. Skills tests are based on the product or outcome of the movement. These product assessments provide objective data and can be useful to teachers. Some skill tests do align well with skills required in various activities and sports. For example, the Modified Dyer Backboard Tennis Test (Hewitt, 1965) has a high correlation with striking abilities required in tennis. One advantage of product-based assessment is the collection of objective data. Students easily can keep count, time or score product-based assessments, allowing teachers to collect data during a single class period. One disadvantage of product-based assessments is the lack of corrective feedback they provide. Feedback is limited to the success of the outcome of the movement and does not take into account the quality of the movement itself. Students can execute the skill incorrectly and still make the basket or hit the target. Product-based assessments are useful tools and provide data for teachers to assess student progress but should be used in combination with some type of qualitative evaluation.

Steps for Creating or Selecting Assessments

Senne and Lund (2012) identified seven steps for developing task-specific rubrics. The following steps are based on their list in the AAHPERD book *Navigating the Program Evaluation Process for PETE & Kinesiology: A Roadmap for Success.*

1. The first step in the process is to review the outcome(s) to be measured or the assignment or task to be evaluated. Based on the outcome or assignment, teachers either select an appropriate assessment(s) or create an assessment specific to the outcome(s) or assignment. A good place to start is to imagine what a quality performance or product would look like and identify criterion behaviors associated with quality performance. Identifying common performance mistakes or misconceptions also is part of the process. The most important question is "Does the assessment

Behavior-Change Plan Assignment Guidelines

Directions for change project:

1. Choose one behavior (target behavior) that you would like to change that is related to either physical activity or nutrient intake. The behavior change should relate to your overall health or wellness. After selecting a target behavior, write a behavior-change goal.

2. Define the goal statement in terms of the desired outcome resulting from the behavior change. State the goal in objective terms and make it measurable and specific. Avoid making a general statement such as "I want to be more active." A goal statement should be defined by behavior and should delineate a timeline for achieving the change. For example, replace the statement "I want to be more active" with "I want to complete 10,000 steps per day at least four days a week over a two-week period."

3. After stating your goal, describe why you want to change the behavior. It's important to connect the "what" you would like to change to the "why" you believe you need to make the change. Identify at least three benefits associated with the behavior change.

4. Decide how you are going to measure and collect data on your identified target behavior. That will require you to collect baseline data for a week before implementing your plan for change. For the goal above, you would track how many steps you take over a seven-day period, and that would establish your baseline. If you average 3,986 steps a day, you then either can make some decisions about how to increase your step count to 10,000 or modify the goal. If the current baseline step count is low, you might need to revise the goal to 8,000 steps. At the end of the week, you will graph your baseline data onto a chart and calculate an average for the week.

5. Identify at least three triggers that might facilitate the behavior change or barriers that might inhibit it. For example, weather or friends who would rather play video games might present a barrier to reaching your 10,000-step target. Once you've identified those triggers or barriers, develop a plan for how to deal with them. Use effective self-management skills to implement the plan.

6. Design and implement a plan for changing the behavior. Using your baseline data, develop a two-week behavior plan that includes a timeline for change. For the example above, you might create a plan to walk a specified number of steps on Monday, Wednesday, Friday and Sunday of the first week to build to the 10,000-step goal.

7. Over the two weeks of the program, collect data on your progress toward meeting the goal. At the end of the two weeks, graph the data and compare final data results with baseline data.

8. Write a two-page reflection on the success of your behavior-change plan. Analyze the data to support any conclusions you have reached about meeting or not meeting your goal. Support all conclusions with examples. Answer the following questions as part of your reflection:

    1. Did you meet your goal? Why or why not? Use examples to support your conclusion.

    2. What barriers did you encounter and how did you overcome them?

    3. What skills or knowledge did you use to change your behavior?

    4. How would you improve your behavior plan? Be specific.

    5. How has your outlook changed based on this experience?

Assessment of the final project will be based on the attached rubric. Common Core State Standards in writing and math are part of the final assessment. Your ability to collect and analyze the data and your written-communication skills are important parts of completing this assignment successfully.

Figure 8.5 Sample outline for behavior change.

Rubric for Behavior-Change Plan

Outcome: Creates and implements a behavior-change plan that enhances a healthy, active lifestyle in college or career settings. (S3.H11.L1)

Criterion	Level 1	Level 2	Level 3
Target behavior and goal Weight = 2 (S3.H11.L1)	Target behavior is appropriate but goal is a general statement of behavior, is not measurable and/or fails to identify a timeline.	Target behavior is appropriate. Goal statement uses an action verb and/or is measurable, establishes a timeline and is specific.	Target behavior is appropriate and represents a challenge. Goal statement is specific, uses an action verb, identifies criteria and establishes a timeline.
What and why Weight = 3 (S3.H11.L1)	Identifies fewer than three benefits of the behavior change. Benefits identified are general and unrelated to target behavior.	Identifies at least three benefits of the behavior change. Benefits are aligned with target behavior.	Identifies three or more benefits of the behavior change that are aligned with goal. Supports each benefit by citing source information.
Measurement and data collection Weight = 5 (S3.H11.L1)	Selected measure does not provide meaningful data or is misaligned with target behavior. Data are graphed incorrectly, or no graph is provided. No average is calculated for each week.	Selected measure is aligned with target behavior. Baseline and final data are graphed correctly. Average for each week is calculated.	Selected measure is aligned with target behavior. Baseline and final data are represented correctly on the same line or bar graph to allow for easy comparison. Average for each week is calculated.
Triggers or barriers and self-management Weight = 4 (S4.H1.L1)	Identifies fewer than three triggers or barriers, or triggers or barriers are not appropriate for target behavior. Self-management plan consists of general statements and lacks specificity.	Identifies three triggers or barriers aligned with target behavior. Develops a self-management plan to overcome identified triggers or behaviors aligned with target behavior.	Identifies three or more triggers or barriers aligned directly with target behaviors. Self-management plan aligns with target behavior and provides specific strategies for overcoming identified triggers or barriers.
Design and implement plan Weight = 8 (S3.H13.L1 or S3.H12.L1)	Plan is appropriate for target behavior but does not align with baseline data (too easy or too difficult). Plan is stated in general terms and lacks specificity. No plan for data collection is identified.	Plan is aligned with analysis of baseline data and is appropriate for target behavior. Plan identifies specific or progressive steps for behavior change and data collection.	Plan is aligned with analysis of baseline data and data are cited to support the plan. Plan is appropriate for target behavior. Plan identifies specific and progressive steps for behavior change and data collection.

Figure 8.6 Sample analytical rubric.

Continued

Criterion	Level 1	Level 2	Level 3
Reflection (Weight = 5) (S3.H11.L1)	Not all questions are addressed in reflection. Reflection consists of generalized statements without supporting examples.	All questions are at least partially addressed and supported by data analysis or specific examples. Conclusions are appropriate.	All questions are addressed fully and supported by data analysis and specific examples. Conclusions are insightful and demonstrate critical thinking.
Writing clarity (Weight = 3)	Submission has numerous (more than 15) spelling or grammar errors. Lacks clarity and fails to use academic language associated with nutrition or health-enhancing fitness.	Submission has 15 or fewer spelling or grammar errors. Plans and reflection are written with clarity and effective use of transitions. Technical language specific to nutrition or health-enhancing fitness is used appropriately.	Submission has fewer than 10 spelling or grammar errors. Plans and reflection are written with clarity and with effective use of transitions and demonstrate command of language specific to nutrition or heath-enhancing fitness.
Data analysis (Weight = 3)	Data are assigned incorrectly on X and Y axes. Conclusions are not supported by the presented data. No attempt is made to compare baseline and final data.	Data are represented correctly on the X and Y axes on one graph. Data analysis is correct. Data comparison between baseline and final data is appropriate.	Data are represented correctly on the X and Y axes on both graphs. Data analysis is correct and logical conclusions are reached based on the data. Data comparison between baseline and final data is appropriate.

Number of points earned _____ divided by 99 possible points equals _____ %.

Figure 8.6 Continued

provide evidence of students' mastery of the outcome and assess the most critical components of the task or assignment?" If the answer is yes, the assessment is a valid measure of the outcome or assignment. The same question applies when using an existing assessment. All selected assessments should be reviewed for alignment to the task or assignment and content validity should be established. That might require an existing assessment to be modified to align directly with the task or assignment.

2. If the decision is made to create an assessment, descriptors are developed. Descriptors must be observable and must describe discrete behaviors aligned with criterion behaviors identified in step 1. If the decision

is to use a checklist or rating scale, descriptors should use parallel language. If a rubric is developed, descriptors can be combined into a list or groupings of words or phrases related to the component to be measured. Determining the number of levels used for the rubric is the next step, with at least three levels and no more than five being the most common choices. Teachers then begin to describe performance criteria for each of the levels. One recommendation is to start with the middle level. After criterion behaviors are identified for the middle level, teachers simply describe criterion performance above and below the middle level.

3. After developing the assessment, teachers should pilot it with a group of students to

determine how well it assesses the outcome(s) or assignment, ease of use and appropriateness of the criterion behaviors identified. Piloting the assessment will allow teachers to discover whether changes or revisions to the assessment are needed.

4. The final steps are to revise the assessment based on the pilot test, develop a data-collection system and implement the assessment.

Strategies for Assessing Large Groups of Students

One of the greatest challenges that physical educators face is assessing and tracking student progress. As noted earlier in this chapter, that challenge is based on the volume of students enrolled in physical education each grading period or year. With physical education teachers tracking the progress of hundreds of students each marking period, they must make some difficult decisions about how often and how much to assess each year.

One of those difficult decisions should be to begin to track data over time for all students. That will require teachers to use technology to both gather and track data. While keeping hundreds of pieces of paper on students is not feasible, tracking progress electronically is. Teachers can use Excel, Google forms, Wiki sites and many other electronic tools to create databases, report student progress and share results with learners, parents and administrators.

Listed here are some practical tips for assessing and tracking student progress over time. Some of these suggestions are adapted from AAHPERD's *PE Metrics* (2010) series, which serves as a valuable resource for teachers for assessing outcomes specific to Standards 1 and 2.

1. Limit the number of assessments completed for the year. Teachers should review grade-level outcomes and determine the most important outcomes to be assessed

based on curriculum and program goals. For example, formally assessing all six motor patterns each year is not a good use of time. These patterns should be formally assessed at the grade level at which a maturing pattern is an expectation. That doesn't eliminate informal assessment before that point, as determining whether students are meeting developmental benchmarks is important. The scope and sequence chart on p. 66 provides a quick reference on grade-level expectations, with developmental benchmarks serving as signposts to the achievement of mature fundamental motor patterns.

2. Try to assess at least one or two outcomes per marking period. Formal assessment of students' progress should be ongoing, with the tracking of progress each marking period.

3. Complete informal assessments daily. They can include peer assessments, checks for understanding, exit slips, quizzes or worksheets.

4. Be creative in working with classroom teachers and parents to help with assessments in physical education. During home-room or free period, students could record fitness data or view a "flipped" classroom video, in which teachers record lessons meant to be viewed outside of regular class time and the lesson is practiced during class time, when the teacher is available for help and guidance. Parents could help children with activity logs through a school-based site or an open site such as Wiki spaces. Suggest that the library or computer room be made available before and after school or during lunch so students can complete electronic assignments in physical education.

5. Use electronic tablets to record data and complete assessments. Set up the tablet so that if no score is recorded, the default is the satisfactory level on the rubric or a check is automatically recorded for the criterion behavior. That will allow you to note only students who are below or above the criterion behaviors. Those students are easy to spot as you observe them during deliberate practice tasks or modified game play. Most students will be at the satisfactory level, which will limit the number of recordings you must complete.

6. Assess small groups of students each class period. You can set up an assessment as a station or during warm-up activities. Assess over the entire unit and not simply at the end of the unit.

7. Share assessment criterion behaviors and assessments with students. Guidelines for completing assessments should be part of the assessment package and posted electronically. Students are more likely to complete the tasks successfully if they know your expectations.

8. Rubrics are easy to use, provide meaningful feedback to students and parents and facilitate the assessment process. You don't have to mark individual sheets for each student; simply record the level achieved on a grade sheet for each component of the rubric. If the rubric has five separate components, the grade sheet has the five components listed at the top and you simply record a number (1-3 or 1-5, depending on the number of levels on the rubric) for each student. Set the middle level as the default and simply mark scores for students performing over or under the middle levels.

9. Note performance errors. Create a numbered list of common performance errors and simply note the number for that error. For example, in the overhand throwing pattern, some of the most common errors are 1) unilateral step (not stepping in opposition), 2) elbow below shoulder, 3) step and turn poorly timed, 4) facing target (not sideways to target) and 5) no full range of motion on the throw. Record the number(s) of the performance error(s) next to the student's name. If no numbers are recorded, the student is demonstrating the critical elements for the overhand throw.

10. Use student aides, parent volunteers and others to help collect and track student data. It's important to work with the assessment coordinator for the school or district to set up an assessment plan. They are valuable resources for developing assessment systems and tracking data.

Summary

Assessment is an essential component of quality physical education. Through preassessment, the foundation is laid for instruction. Through ongoing formative assessment, the teacher and students know how well learning is progressing. And through summative assessment, teachers can share evidence of student learning with students, parents and administrators. With assessment data, teachers can track student progress across grade levels and provide evidence of program effectiveness and value. Teachers also can demonstrate that students are meeting standards and outcomes and thus, advocate for their programs. Although integrating assessment into physical education can be challenging, it clearly is the most valuable tool in the teacher's toolkit.

Chapter 9

Resources for Teaching
the Standards & Outcomes

Helena Baert
State University of New York at Cortland

Joey Feith
Royal Charles Elementary School and founder of ThePhysicalEducator.com

Physical educators have a multitude of resources available to them for enhancing their pedagogical skill set. These resources include traditional materials such as books and journal articles as well as professional-development opportunities such as conferences, workshops and webinars. In addition, the number of websites related to physical education continues to expand, providing venues for sharing ideas and staying abreast of new developments in the field. Any list of these websites or opportunities would quickly be out of date and, thus, is not included here. However, it's important for physical educators to stay connected with physical education-related websites, especially those of their professional organizations (e.g., SHAPE America), so that they can deliver the best possible instructional experience for their students.

Similarly, new technologies are becoming available all the time that physical educators can use as effective instructional tools, and it's essential for teachers to integrate these technologies into their skill sets and classrooms. Rather than presenting specific instructional technologies, which would be obsolete in short order, this chapter provides guidance on how to use technology to enhance teaching and students' attainment of grade-level outcomes. The second part of the chapter provides resources that are available from SHAPE America to support teachers in using appropriate instructional practices and developing standards-based curricula and assessments.

Using Technology to Teach the Standards & Outcomes

The goal of the National Standards & Grade-Level Outcomes for K-12 Physical Education is to develop physically literate individuals who are confident in their abilities and knowledge so that they will become lifelong movers. The standards and outcomes provide a framework through which to guide instructional decision making and identify developmental benchmarks. While the framework is helpful in developing a scope and sequence, teachers are now confronted with the tasks of creating learning experiences, deciding on which teaching approaches and tools to use and developing assessments that track progress over time. These are all part of the instructional decision-making process, with students at the center of that process.

While the National Standards provide a framework, each teaching experience and class is unique. Teachers use their knowledge of students to select and create learning experiences that are specific to the needs of those students. Once those needs are determined, teachers dig into their bags of instructional tools and strategies and select those that will facilitate learning. One of the tools in that bag is technology. While some physical educators are very familiar with various technology applications, others might wonder where to start or even whether it's

necessary to use technology at all. This chapter is focused on how teachers can use technology as a tool for creating positive change in physical education and meeting grade-level outcomes. It identifies key points to examine when considering the use of technology as a learning tool for physical education.

Why Use Technology in Physical Education?

Technology is an integral part of teaching and learning in 21st century schools. This technology revolution has affected all disciplines and subject areas. Many physical educators do recognize the potential benefits that technology integration can have on teaching and learning and have found many uses for its application. For example, physical educators use pedometers to help students keep track of movement, heart rate monitors to enhance students' training potential and video to observe, analyze and improve students' skill performance. Pedometers and heart rate monitors enhance students' attainment of outcomes in Standard 3 (engages in physical activity and fitness knowledge) at the middle school (e.g., S3.M8.8) and high school (e.g., S3.H10.L2) levels. In addition, mobile applications help teachers take attendance, keep track of grades and minimize time

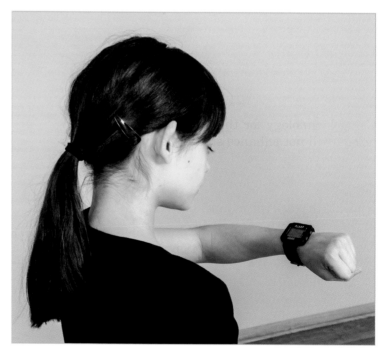

spent on management tasks while allowing more time for instruction, deliberate practice and assessment.

Those are only a few examples of technology use. New tools appear every day, mandating that physical educators understand the reasoning and process of selecting appropriate technology based on the principles of effective instruction. Once those principles are understood, technology in physical education can benefit both the learner and the teacher by enhancing learning and increasing teaching effectiveness.

Teachers should never feel pressured to use the newest tools, which might or might not be appropriate and actually could impair student learning or overwhelm the teacher. Teachers should not use technology if it inhibits learning or distracts from the learning process. As the National Association for Sport and Physical Education (2009) notes, "The use of instructional technology in physical education is designed to supplement, not substitute for, effective instruction" (p. 3).

The following four principles provide guidance to teachers on the appropriate uses of technology to enhance student learning and increase teaching effectiveness. Technology should be used

1. As a tool (just like a beanbag or badminton racket).
2. As a supplement to—not a substitute for—instruction.
3. To enhance learning.
4. To enhance teaching effectiveness.

Using Technology as a Tool

Using technology for the sake of using technology will not enhance student learning and actually might have the opposite effect. For example, pedometers are great tools for a walking or jogging unit in which the objective is for students to track the number of steps they take and then use that information to increase their activity levels (S3.M8.8). But using pedometers in a yoga unit will not produce data that are meaningful for objectives related to increasing flexibility or reducing stress (S3.M18.8). Instructional decisions about the use of technology tools should be driven by the objectives of the unit and lesson.

The same decision-making process applies to the many new mobile applications that show great potential for teachers. The latest mobile application shouldn't dictate what is taught or how the class is run, but it should afford physical education teachers more opportunities to select effective tools that enhance instruction.

Using Technology as a Supplement to Instruction

It's not about the tool! Teaching is a process of decision making. Physical educators make decisions based on their students' experiences and abilities while adhering to the standards and learning objectives as described in a scope and sequence. The instructional cycle in figure 9.1 will keep learning in the forefront. It illustrates how technology is never first but rather should be used as a supplemental tool that supports learning.

Step 1. Identify

- From the curriculum and scope and sequence, identify the grade-level outcomes to be addressed.
- Identify the skills and concepts that students should be able to do and know to meet the grade-level outcomes.
- Identify the central focus of your lesson.
- Identify the key lesson objectives.

Step 2. Select

- Select developmentally appropriate learning tasks to align with selected grade-level outcomes and objectives.
- Select appropriate instructional supports (includes technology, teaching styles and equipment).
- Select the appropriate learning environment.
- Select assessments that provide evidence of student learning.

Step 3. Plan

- Decide how you will manage the lessons.
- When using technology, you will need to set up routines, teach protocols and scaffold technology integration to ensure that

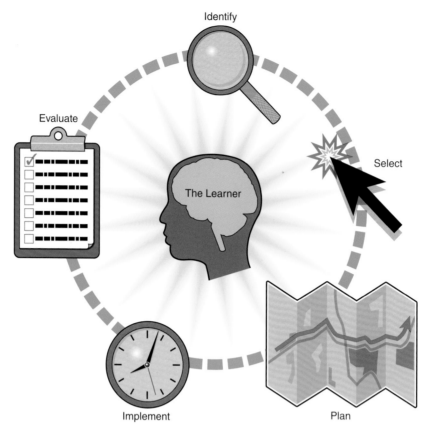

Figure 9.1 Instructional cycle.

the use of technology strengthens the learning process.

• Create your unit or lesson plan.

Step 4. Implement

• Carry out your plan; deliver your lesson.
• Record results and collect evidence of student learning.

Step 5. Evaluate

• Reflect on the implementation of the lesson and the usefulness of the instructional tools.
• Adjust your next plan when necessary.

Central: The Learner

• In every step, keep the learner in mind.
• Use your knowledge of your students when selecting learning tasks, instructional supports and assessments.
• Preassess your students on their skills, knowledge and ability to use technology.
• Plan your lessons with your students in mind.

Using Technology to Enhance Learning

As the previous section suggests, learning should always be at the forefront. Simply adopting a technology tool is not enough. With any instructional tool, teachers must create progressive and appropriate learning experiences for students when using the technology. For example, when teaching young students how to throw underhand (S1.E13.K), a physical educator would not give kindergarten students a ball. The teacher, instead, would start with using bean bags to help students understand and grasp the fundamental motor skill and, depending on students' abilities and speed of learning, would progressively change the equipment as appropriate. Students would progress from a bean bag to a small ball to a larger, lighter ball and, finally, to a heavier ball at the middle school level (S1.M18.6). The same goes for implementing technology. Students enter the gymnasium with various experiences in using technology. Because the focus should not be on the tool but rather on the learning, teachers must integrate technology carefully so that it strengthens learning and never takes away from the learning process. When technology takes over, learning will suffer. It's necessary, therefore, for teachers to scaffold the integration of technology, keeping in mind students' previous experiences with that technology.

To understand the process of scaffolding and appropriate sequencing, here are some suggestions for scaffolding students' use of video analysis in physical education.

Elementary School

- Teacher video-records a skill performance. Students view one critical element together, then students and teacher discuss the critical element

- Teacher demonstrates use of a flip camera to students so that they learn to start and stop recording and review video.

- In partners, one student video-records while the partner performs. Then, students view one critical element together.

- In partners, one student video-records while the partner performs. Then, partners use checklist, discuss and perform again (supports S4.E4.5).

Middle School

- Teacher teaches video-recording protocols.
- Students can use a flip camera to record and analyze an entire skill (three critical elements).
- Students experiment with peer analysis and self-analysis (supports S4.M3.7).
- Students experiment with mobile apps for video analysis.

High School

Students use video analysis for

- Peer assessment and self-assessment (supports S2.H2.L1),
- Reflection and self-planning,
- Connecting performance to training,
- Analyzing game play,
- Creating and editing videos and
- Inclusion in a personal portfolio.

Using Technology to Enhance Teaching Effectiveness

As stated previously, many technological tools available today can help teachers increase their efficiency in different aspects of teaching, including facilitating student learning, planning, managing and professional development. Mobile devices, cloud-supported applications and social media are just some examples.

Mobile Devices

Modern mobile devices (e.g., smart phones, tablets) allow teachers to carry and access a variety of tools such as cameras, computers, web browsers, timers and video players, all in a small—sometimes pocket size—form. Based on their portability and functionality, mobile devices allow teachers to access the tools they need instantly, provide immediate feedback to the student and capture evidence of student learning in authentic settings.

Cloud-Supported Applications

Advancements in web-based technologies now allow users to synchronize their applications across several devices via the cloud (i.e., the app syncs to an external server via the Internet and any changes will appear on any other device on

which the user has installed the app). Having information synchronized and stored in the cloud allows teachers to access that information from any Internet-enabled device. Even if a teacher loses or misplaces his or her device, the teacher still can access the information he or she has saved by signing into the account through another device. In most applications, this information can be organized and accessed easily. Also, because the information is stored digitally on a server, it can be shared easily through communication services such as e-mail and instant messaging. Allowing teachers to have constant, easy access to all of the information they need can help them save time and focus on their teaching.

Social Media

Teachers around the world now use social media as a tool for professional development. Social media sites have allowed teachers to grow their professional networks and have provided them with a platform through which they can share and develop their ideas. Sharing, networking and collaborating online leads to an increase in professional-development opportunities for teachers, which in turn allows them to develop their teaching skills on a more regular basis and stay up to date with current trends in physical education. Students also can use social media and other technologies as tools for supporting a healthy lifestyle (S3.H2.L2).

Technology as an Obstacle to Teaching Efficiency

Although technology—when used appropriately—can help teachers teach more efficiently, physical educators must be careful to make sure that the tool doesn't become a distraction that gets in the way of learning. For example, during a lesson on basketball (S1.M10.6) the teacher might notice that one student is not aligning his elbow with the net when performing a free throw. To help the student improve his technique, the teacher decides to use a video analysis application on a tablet device. The teacher informs the student about the application, records the student's performance, analyzes the video with the student and then makes the recommendation to align

the elbow with the net before taking the shot. Although technology might have helped the student improve his technique in this situation, a faster and perhaps more efficient way of doing so might have been to simply provide the student with a simple learning cue (e.g., "Pull your elbow in before taking the shot"). In this situation, the teacher's enthusiasm for the technology became a distraction to the learning process.

Choosing the Right Technology

While technology can be a distraction, it's important to remember that technology can, indeed, help enhance teaching when used as a tool for completing a teaching-management task efficiently. All teachers have encountered challenging management tasks. Table 9.1 lists a few examples of these tasks, as well as examples of traditional methods of completing the tasks, distracting uses of technology and efficient uses of technology in carrying out these management tasks.

When deciding whether to use a traditional method of classroom management or use technology, remember that the efficiency of either option depends on the teacher. For example, although some teachers might have great handwriting and are very organized in their notes, other teachers struggle with the process of writing notes by hand. Therefore, having typed, digital, searchable notes might be a more efficient option for certain teachers. In addition, teachers should take into account their own preferences and skills when choosing whether to use traditional methods or technology when it comes to completing classroom-management tasks.

Accessibility Issues

Another factor that teachers must take into consideration is accessibility to the technology. For example, a teacher decides to create a blog through which she will deliver handouts, course information and review materials. Although the teacher's intentions were good, he or she might not have taken into consideration the fact that some students might not have Internet access outside of school. Although the class blog

Table 9.1 Using Technology to Streamline Teaching-Management Tasks

Teaching-management tasks	Examples of traditional methods	Examples of distracting uses of technology	Examples of efficient uses of technology
Keeping track of attendance	Pen–paper solutions These records can easily be lost, misplaced, or destroyed.	Spreadsheet on desktop computer Keeping attendance records using a spreadsheet forces teachers to be at a computer while taking attendance. Also—similar to the pen–paper solution—if the computer fails, the records are lost.	Mobile attendance application Using an app that syncs to an online server allows teachers to take attendance while moving around the gym and to keep and access those records from any Internet-enabled device.
Collecting evidence of student learning. Portfolios are an important component of achieving the outcomes in Standard 3 for middle and high school students.	Binder portfolios Binder portfolios are difficult to keep organized, can hold only physical documents, require a lot of space to store and can be destroyed easily.	Digital USB portfolios. Although USBs allow the teacher to include a variety of media (e.g., documents, pictures, videos) within the portfolio, this system requires each student to have his or her own USB, be careful not to lose it, and bring it to and from class every time the teacher wishes to update it. Also, to capture said media, the teacher would need a variety of devices (e.g., camera, audio recorder, scanner).	Mobile portfolio application Mobile devices allow teachers to capture evidence of student learning through a variety of media, all with the same device. Certain mobile applications then allow the teacher to store and organize this evidence into portfolios via the cloud (i.e., on an external server through the Internet). Portfolios then can be shared with students and parents through a variety of means, including e-mail.

might make the teacher's task of distributing course materials easier to manage, he or she must remember to select tools that all students will be able to access and use.

Summary

Every day, new tools become available, and often the novelty of such tools can be overwhelming to busy teachers. It's important to remember that technology is a tool that supplements instruction; it does not drive instruction. No matter where you start, take it slow and start small. A common suggestion is to look at what you are teaching and what students are learning and try one tool at a time. Then, take the time to use it, teach with it and evaluate its usefulness before trying a different tool.

When deciding on a technology to use, ask yourself the following two questions:

1. Does it enhance learning?

2. Does it increase the effectiveness of my teaching?

If the answer to both questions is "No," either don't use the tool or allow more time for its implementation to be questioned and evaluated further. Because, after all, it's not about the tool!

SHAPE America Resources for Teaching to the Standards & Outcomes

The Society of Health and Physical Educators (SHAPE America) offers numerous resources to assist practitioners with appropriate instructional practices as well as with developing standards-based curricula and assessments that will help implement the National Standards & Grade-Level Outcomes for K-12 Physical Education.

Visit www.aahperd.org to find information about SHAPE America books, as well as to download free copies of position statements and guidance documents on various topics of interest to physical educators, including *Appropriate Instructional Practice Guidelines* and *Opportunity to Learn Guidelines* for elementary, middle and high school.

The following is a sample listing of these resources, which will support teachers in implementing the standards and outcomes.

National Standards & Grade-Level Outcomes

Smart PE Moves for Middle School Students: Ready-to-Use Lesson Plans & Assessment Tools for Standards-Based Physical Education (2012)

PE Metrics: Assessing National standards 1-6 in Secondary School (2011)

PE Metrics: Assessing National Standards 1-6 in Elementary School (2010)

Flash Fitness & the Incredible Physical Activities: A Super-Hero Approach to Meeting the National PE Standards in Grades K-5 (2010)

Concepts and Principles of Physical Education: What Every Student Needs to Know (2010)

Movement-Based Learning for Children: Academic Concepts and Physical Activity for Ages 3-8 (2006)

Physical Activity for Children: A Statement of Guidelines for Children Ages 5-12 (2004)

Appropriate Instructional Practice

Appropriate Instructional Practice Guidelines for Elementary School Physical Education (2009)

Appropriate Instructional Practice Guidelines for Middle School Physical Education (2009)

Appropriate Instructional Practice Guidelines for High School Physical Education (2009)

Opportunity to Learn

Opportunity to Learn Guidelines for Elementary School Physical Education (2009)

Opportunity to Learn Guidelines for Middle School Physical Education (2009)

Opportunity to Learn Guidelines for High School Physical Education (2009)

SHAPE America Assessment Series

Assessment for Everyone: Modifying NASPE Assessments to Include All Elementary School Children (2011)

Assessing and Improving Fitness in Elementary Physical Education (2008)

Standards-Based Assessment of Student Learning: A Comprehensive Approach (2007)

Assessing Dance in Elementary Physical Education (2005)

Assessment of Swimming in Physical Education (2005)

Assessing Concepts: Secondary Biomechanics (2004)

Assessment in Outdoor Adventure Physical Education (2003)

Assessing Student Outcomes in Sport Education (2003)

Authentic Assessment of Physical Activity for High School Students (2002)

Creating Rubrics for Physical Education (2000)

Assessing Motor Skills in Elementary Physical Education (1999)

Assessment in Games Teaching (1999)

Position Statements

Physical Education Is Critical to Educating the Whole Child (2011)

Appropriate Uses of Fitness Measurement (2010)

Appropriate Use of Instructional Technology in Physical Education (2009)

Appropriate Maximum Class Length for Elementary Physical Education (2008)

About the Chapter 9 Contributors

Helena Baert, PhD, is assistant professor of physical education at State University of New York, Cortland. Her research interests include the evaluation of appropriate integration of technology within K-12 physical education and physical education teacher-education programs  to enhance learning and teaching, faculty development, linking assessment and technology, and fitness and technology. Baert teaches undergraduate- and graduate-level courses in elementary and secondary physical education, curriculum and instruction, leadership and technology.

Joey Feith is a physical education teacher from Montreal, Canada. In 2010, he founded The-PhysicalEducator.com, an online resource that aims to help physical educators improve their teaching practices through innovative ideas, high-quality  resources and professional-development opportunities. Feith has presented his ideas on the application of technology in physical education at the international level.

Glossary

Accuracy—For the purposes of this book, reasonable accuracy is defined as 60 percent successful performance; accuracy is 80 percent or above. Scores in the range of 60 percent to 79 percent are considered reasonably accurate.

Affective domain—The domain in which the focus is on personal–social development, attitudes, values, feelings, motivation and emotions. In the revised Bloom's taxonomy (Anderson et al., 2005), affective behaviors include receiving (willing to listen and hear), responding (willing to participate actively), valuing (willing to be involved, accept and commit), organizing (willing to advocate and synthesize) and characterization (willing to change behavior, revise judgments and cooperate).

Analytic rubric—An assessment and instructional tool that divides assignments or tasks into independent component parts with criterion behaviors defined for each part and across levels of the rubric. Each part is evaluated separately across levels, and learners receive feedback for each component part of the assignment or task. The assessment occurs on a continuum defined by criterion behaviors unique to each component.

Applying—Learners can demonstrate the critical elements of the motor skills or knowledge components of the grade-level outcomes in a variety of physical activity environments.

Aquatics—Might include but are not limited to swimming, diving, synchronized swimming and water polo.

Checklist—An assessment and instructional tool that evaluates whether individual performance criteria are present or absent. It consists of a list of criterion behaviors, and evaluators simply determine yes, the criterion behavior is present or no, the criterion behavior is not present. This type of assessment does not attempt to determine the quality of the response.

Closed skills—See entry for **nondynamic environment.**

Cognitive domain—Domain in which the focus is on knowledge and information (facts and concepts), with an emphasis on the understanding and application of knowledge and information through higher-order thinking skills. The revised Bloom's taxonomy (Anderson et al., 2005) identifies six levels of intellectual behaviors (remembering, understanding, applying, analyzing, evaluating and creating), with increasing complexity at each level.

Competency—Sufficient ability, skill and knowledge to meet the demands of a specific task or activity. In this book, competency is defined as the ability for individuals to participate at the recreational level with skill and ability in self-selected activities.

Competitive advantage—The advantage gained in a game situation when one team, either on offense or defense, has more players than the other team. *Example:* When two offensive players are against one defender, the team with two players has a competitive (offensive) advantage. If two offensive players face three defenders, the defense has a competitive advantage.

Content standard—"A statement that . . . clearly describe(s) the content that should be taught and learned during the K-12 years, grade by grade. Content standards articulate an essential core of knowledge and skills that students should master. Standards clarify what students are expected to know and be able to do at various points in their K-12 academic career." Available: www.intime.uni.edu/model/content/cont.html.

Contextual interference effect—Certain conditions (e.g., varying practice tasks) that depress performance during practice but actually produce higher levels of learning and retention (Schmidt & Wrisberg, 2008, p. 258).

Criterion-referenced performance standards—A type of assessment tool that compares learners' performance with a predetermined set of criteria or standard. Criteria are defined clearly, are delimited and are task-specific.

Critical elements—The key components of a motor skill that can be observed, the sum of which result in movement efficiency.

Dance and rhythmic activities—Activities that focus on dance or rhythms. Dance and rhythmic activities might include but are not limited to dance forms such as creative movement, ballet, modern, ethnic or folk, cultural, hip hop, Latin, line, ballroom, social and square. Rhythmic activities for early elementary focus on recognizing and moving to rhythm. Rhythmic manipulative activities for elementary include, but are not limited to, lummi sticks, tinikling, Chinese ribbons and ball gymnastics.

Deliberate practice—Defined as ". . . a highly structured activity, the explicit goal of which is to improve performance. Specific tasks are invented to overcome weaknesses, and performance is carefully monitored to provide cues for ways to improve further" (Ericsson et al., 1993, p. 368). Deliberate practice is purposeful and requires concentration on the part of the learner.

Differentiated instruction—Teachers vary instruction to address the needs of students and their various levels of skill or knowledge. Teachers differentiate instruction by modifying the learning environment (e.g., tiered learning activities), providing choices on equipment (e.g., increasing or decreasing the length of a racket), providing choices on the process (e.g., participate in modified game play or continue to practice), modifying practice (e.g., working alone or in a group) and facilitating self-directed activities (e.g., developing and implementing an individualized physical activity program).

Dynamic environments (open skills)—Skills performed in an environment that is dynamic, unpredictable and in motion. The goal for performers is to adapt movements in response to the dynamic and ever-changing environment (Schmidt & Wrisberg, 2008, p. 9). Examples include invasion games such as ultimate and soccer and net/wall games such as volleyball and tennis.

Educational gymnastics—Focuses on children challenging themselves to maneuver their bodies effectively against the force of gravity (Graham et al., 2013). The skills of balancing and transferring weight form the foundation of educational gymnastics. Educational gymnastics centers on challenges appropriate for each child and his or her skill level, as contrasted with Olympic gymnastics, which centers on defined stunts performed the same way by all students.

Emerging—Learners participate in deliberate practice tasks that will lead to skill and knowledge acquisition. Learners are in the beginning stages of acquiring motor skills and knowledge. Mastery of the skills and knowledge is emerging through deliberate practice tasks and, at this stage, learners are developing competency.

Etiquette—Expectations regarding behavior and social norms associated with specific games or activities; rules of behavior that define and provide parameters for the appropriate participation in the activity or game.

Fielding/striking games—Games in which teams occupy positions throughout the space (field) and the other team tries to score by batting or striking an object into open space in the field, providing enough time for the hitter to run between bases (or wickets). Examples include baseball, softball and cricket. Strategies and tactics include effective placement of field players so that they can prevent scoring (defending team) and batting and striking the object with appropriate power to open spaces in the field (offensive team) (Haibach et al., 2011, p. 365; Mitchell, Oslin & Griffin, 2006, p. 21). Fielding decisions are based on the fielders' position and game situation, such as offensive runners' positions, outs and score.

Fitness activities—Activities with a focus on improving or maintaining fitness that might include yoga, Pilates, resistance training, spinning, running, fitness walking, fitness swimming, kickboxing, cardio–kick, Zumba and exergaming.

FITT—Acronym that stands for frequency, intensity, time and type, which are variables that are manipulated to create an overload.

Fundamental motor skills—The locomotor, nonlocomotor or stability, and manipulative skills that provide the foundation for the more complex and sport-specific movement patterns used in games and sports.

Games and sports—Includes the following game categories: invasion, net/wall, target and fielding/striking.

Grid activities—Grids are squares or rectangles in which learners participate in modified game play using predetermined tactics or skills. For example, learners could practice such skills as give and go with a partner within a grid. The passer passes (gives) to a receiver and moves to another portion of the grid (goes) to receive a return pass. The sequence of passing (give) and moving to a new space in the grid (go) would be repeated for a predetermined amount of time (e.g., 45 seconds) with partners tracking the number of completed passes. Grids can vary in many ways, including size and shape, number of players within the grid and with or without defensive pressure.

Holistic rubric or holistic rating scale—An assessment and instructional tool that assigns a level of performance based on multiple criteria and evaluates the performance as a whole. Learners must demonstrate all the identified criterion behaviors at a particular level for evaluators to determine whether the level has been achieved. Like all rubrics, holistic rubrics must define at least two levels.

Individual-performance activities—Might include gymnastics, figure skating, track and field, multisport events, in-line skating, wrestling, self-defense and skateboarding.

Invasion games—Games in which "teams score by moving a ball (or a projectile) into another team's territory and either shooting into a fixed target (a goal or a basket) or moving the projectile across an open-ended target (a line). To prevent scoring, one team must stop the other from bringing the ball into its territory and attempting to score" (Mitchell et al., 2006). Strategies and tactics include using teammates to open space on offense (with or without the ball) and reduce space on defense. Decision making for offense includes when to pass, carry the ball, shoot and move to create open space. Defenders must decide which players to cover and when to move to reduce space. Examples are basketball, ultimate and soccer.

Inverted position—Balances and transfers of weight in educational gymnastics in which the head is lower than the hips.

Jab step—An offensive skill executed by stepping sharply with one foot toward an opponent to cause the opponent to hesitate or go backward, thereby creating space for the offensive player.

Knowledge of performance—Feedback based on the process and quality of the movement. The feedback is based on movement efficiency, timing and rhythm of the movement pattern. Feedback is provided on specific critical elements of the movement (Schmidt & Wrisberg, 2008, p. 289).

Knowledge of results—Feedback based on the outcome (product) of the movement that occurs after the action is completed (e.g., basket made or missed). Results indicate the degree of the success of the movement based on the environmental goal of the movement (Schmidt & Wrisberg, 2008, p. 286).

Level 1 outcomes—High school-level outcomes reflecting the minimum knowledge and skills that students must acquire and attain by graduation to be college- or career-ready.

Level 2 outcomes—High school-level outcomes that build on Level 1 competencies by augmenting knowledge and skills considered desirable for college or career readiness.

Lifetime activities—Activities that are suitable for participation across the life span and that one can undertake alone or with a partner as opposed to a team. For the purposes of this book, lifetime activities include the categories of outdoor pursuits, selected individual-performance activities, aquatics and net/wall and target games.

Locomotor skills—Skills that "consist of a group of fundamental motor skills that allow individuals to navigate through space or move their body from one point to another." These include "running, galloping, hopping, skipping, jumping, leaping and sliding" (Gallahue et al., 2012, p. 223).

Manipulative skills—Skills that require controlling or manipulating objects, such as kicking, striking, throwing, catching and dribbling.

Mature pattern—Executing with efficiency the critical elements of the motor skills pattern in authentic environments.

Maturing—Demonstrating the critical elements of the motor skills and knowledge components of the grade-level outcomes, which will continue to be refined with practice. As the environmental context varies, a maturing pattern might fluctuate, reflecting more maturity in familiar contexts and less maturity in unfamiliar (new) contexts.

Modified games—Small-sided games in which the rules have been modified to emphasize the skills taught in class (e.g., creating a penalty for dribbling to emphasize teaching students to pass rather than dribble).

Motor patterns—The six fundamental motor skills are running, jumping and landing, kicking, throwing, catching and striking. These skills provide the foundation for more complex and sport-specific movement patterns used in games and sports.

Movement concepts—The application of knowledge and concepts related to skillful performance of movement and fitness activities, such as spatial awareness, effort, tactics, strategies and principles related to movement efficiency and health-enhancing fitness.

Net/wall games—Games in which "teams or individual players score by hitting a ball into a court space with sufficient accuracy and power so that opponents cannot hit it back before it bounces once (as in badminton or volleyball) or twice (as in tennis or racquetball)" (Mitchell et al., 2006, p. 21). Opponents generally are separated by a net, but in some cases (squash, racquetball), they share a court and the walls are in play. Offensive strategies and tactics are based on hitting to an open space or pulling the opponent out of position. Defensive strategies are reducing open space by good court position and anticipating the opponent's shot.

Nondynamic environment (closed skills)—Skills performed in a nondynamic environment that is constant, predictable or stationary. The goal for performers is to produce movements or skills that are consistent and accurate because the environmental context is nondynamic, stable and unchanging (Schmidt & Wrisberg, 2008, p. 9). Examples include performance sports such as gymnastics or diving and target games such as darts and archery.

Nonlocomotor or stability skills—"Any movement that places a premium on gaining and maintaining one's equilibrium in relation to the force of gravity" (Gallahue et al., 2012, p. 49). Examples include axial movements (another term sometimes used for nonlocomotor movements) as well as inverted and rolling body postures.

Norm-referenced—A type of assessment tool that compares learners' performance with other similar learners' performances. Learners' relative standing (rank) is based on their performance in comparison with other similar learners in the same age group.

Outcomes—Statements that specify what learners will know or be able to do as a result of a learning activity.

Outdoor pursuits—Activities that include recreational boating (e.g., kayaking, canoeing, sailing, rowing); hiking; backpacking; fishing; orienteering or geocaching; ice skating; skateboarding; snow or water skiing; snowboarding; snowshoeing; surfing; bouldering, traversing or climbing; mountain biking; adventure activities; and ropes courses. Selection of activities is dependent on the environmental opportunities within the geographical region.

Overload principle—Progressively placing greater stress or demands on the body during exercise to cause the body to adapt (become more fit). This is accomplished by manipulating the frequency, intensity, time (duration) and type (FITT) of activity.

Player up or player down—A game situation in which one team has one more (e.g., 2v1) or one fewer (e.g., 1v2) player than the other team.

Psychomotor domain—Domain in which focus is on motor skills. "Includes physical movement, coordination and the use of the motor-skill areas. Development of these skills requires practice and is measured in terms of speed, precision, distance, procedures or techniques in execution" (Simpson, 1972).

Rating scale—An assessment and instructional tool that is similar to a checklist but provides added information on the extent to which criterion behaviors are met. That is accomplished by a gradation of criteria across levels. Gradation of performance can be differentiated by the number of times the behavior occurs (frequency) or by descriptions of performance at each level (quality).

Receiving—The skill of collecting a pass from a teammate with the hands, feet or body.

Rubric—An assessment and instructional tool that identifies criterion behaviors for at least two levels of performance. Each level of the rubric identifies and describes criterion behaviors that contain essential elements of the tasks along a range or continuum of performance expectations.

Small-sided games—Organized games in which the number of players involved is reduced from the conventional competitive version of the sport (e.g., 2v2 basketball, 3v3 volleyball, 6v6 lacrosse).

Small-sided practice tasks—Small-sided games or deliberate tasks designed to practice particular skills or tasks.

Striking—"A ballistic, propulsion skill . . . with several forms, such as sidearm, underarm or overarm, one-handed and two-handed" (Gallahue et al., 2012, p. 214). Common examples include batting, hitting with a racket and serving a volleyball.

Target games—Games in which "players score by throwing or striking an object to a target" (Mitchell et al., 2006, p. 21). Accuracy is a primary focus of the activity, and competitors share no physical contact (Haibach et al., 2011, p. 369). Target games are considered opposed (e.g., croquet, shuffleboard, bocce) because opponents may block or hit another player's ball to a less-desirable position. Other target games are considered unopposed (e.g., golf, bowling) because opponents may not interfere with a shot (Mitchell et al., 2006, p. 21). Strategies or tactics are based on movement accuracy and consistency.

Technology—Software, websites, devices and applications used in a physical education setting to enhance teaching and learning.

Volley—To strike or give impetus to an object (volleybirds, foot bags, bamboo balls, volleyballs) by using a variety of body parts (e.g., hands, arms, head, knees) (Graham et al., 2013).

Bibliography

Anderson, L.W., Krathwohl, D.R., & Bloom, B.S. (2005). *A taxonomy for learning, teaching, and assessing.* New York: Longman.

Azzarito, L., & Solmon, M. (2009). An investigation of students' embodied discourses in physical education: A gender project. *Journal of Teaching in Physical Education, 28,* 173–191.

Balestracci, K. (2013). Benefits and implementation: A fitness for life, physical component, and nutrition unit. In L.E. Ciccomascolo & E.C. Sullivan (Eds.), *The dimensions of physical education* (pp. 143–152). Burlington, MA: Jones & Bartlett Learning.

Barnett, L.M., van Beurden, E., Morgan, P.J., Brooks, L.O., & Beard, J.R. (2010). Gender differences in motor skill proficiency from childhood to adolescence: A longitudinal study. *Research Quarterly for Exercise and sport, 81* (2), 162–170.

Barnett, L.M., van Beurden, E., Morgan, P.J., Brooks, L.O., & Beard, J.R. (2008a). Childhood motor skill proficiency as a predictor of adolescent physical activity. *Journal of Adolescent Health, 44,* 252–259.

Barnett, L.M., van Beurden, E., Morgan, P.J., Brooks, L.O., & Beard, J.R. (2008b). Does childhood motor skill proficiency predict adolescent fitness? *Medicine and Science in Sports and Exercise, 40,* 2137–2144.

Basch, C. (2010). Healthier students are better learners: A missing link in school reforms to close the achievement gap. *Equity Matters: Research Review No. 6.* New York: Columbia University.

Bengoechea, E.G., Sabiston, C.M., Ahmed, R., & Farnoush, M. (2010). Exploring links to unorganized and organized physical activity during adolescence: The role of gender, socioeconomic status, weight status, and enjoyment of physical education. *Research Quarterly for Exercise and Sport, 81* (1), 7–16.

Bernstein, E., Phillips, S.R., & Silverman, S. (2011). Attitudes and perceptions of middle school students toward competitive activities in physical education. *Journal of Teaching in Physical Education, 30,* 69–83.

Bevans, K., Fitzpatrick, L., Sanchez, B., & Forest, C.B. (2010). Individual and instructional determinant of student engagement in physical education. *Journal of Teaching in Physical Education, 29,* 399–416.

Board on Science Education (July, 2011). *A framework for k–12 science education: Practices, cross-cutting concepts, and core ideas.* Washington, DC: National Academies Press.

Bradley, C.B., McMurray, R.G., Harrell, J.S., & Deng, S. (2000). Changes in common activities of grade 3 through 10th graders: The CHIC Study. *Medicine and Science in Sports and Exercise, 32* (12), 2071–2078.

Bryan, C., Sims, S., Hester, D., & Dunaway, D. (2013). Fifteen years after the Surgeon General's Report: Challenges, changes, and future directions in physical education. *Quest, 65,* 139–150.

Buck, M., Lund, J., Harrison, J., & Blakemore Cook, C. (2005). *Instructional strategies for secondary school physical education with NASPE.* New York: McGraw-Hill.

Capio, C.M., Sit, C.H., Abernethy, B., & Masters, R.S. (2012). Fundamental movement skills and physical activity among children with and without cerebral palsy. *Research in Developmental Disabilities, 33* (4), 1235–1241.

Carlson, T. (1995). We hate gym: Student alienation from physical education. *Journal of Teaching in Physical Education, 14,* 467–477.

Castelli, D.M., & Valley, J.A. (2007). Chapter three: The relationship of physical fitness and motor competence to physical activity. *Journal of Teaching in Physical Education, 26,* 358–374.

Charness, N. (1981). Search in chess: Age and skilled differences. *Journal of Experimental Psychology: Human Perception and Performance, 7,* 467–476.

Chen, S., Chen, A., & Zhu, X. (2012). Are k–12 learners motivated in physical education? A meta-analysis. *Research Quarterly for Exercise and Sport, 83* (1), 36–48.

Chen, A., & Darst, P.W. (2001). Situational interest in physical education: A function of learning task design. *Research Quarterly for Exercise and Sport, 72* (2), 150–164.

Chepko, S., & Arnold, R. (Eds.). (2000). *Guidelines for physical education programs: Grades k–12 standards, objectives, and assessments.* Boston: Allyn & Bacon.

Clark, J.E. (2007). On the problem of motor skill development. Speech delivered at AAHPERD Convention, Baltimore, MD.

Clark, J.E., & Metcalfe, J.S. (1997). The mountain of motor development: A metaphor. In J.E. Clark & J. Humphrey (Eds.), *Motor development: Research and reviews, 2* (pp. 8–31). Reston, VA: NASPE.

Clark, J.E., & Metcalfe, J.S. (2002). The mountain of motor development: A metaphor. In J.E. Clark & J. Humphrey (Eds.), *Motor development: Research and reviews, 2* (pp. 163–190). Reston, VA: NASPE.Common Core State Standards Initiative. (2010a). *Common core state standards for English language arts, literacy in history/social studies, science and technical subjects.* Available: www.corestandards.org/.

Common Core State Standards Initiative. (2010a). *Common core state standards for English Language Arts, literacy in History/Social Studies, Science and Technical Subjects.* Retrieved from www.corestandards.org/.

Common Core State Standards Initiative. (2010b). *Common core state standards for mathematics.* Available: www.corestandards.org/.

Corbin, C.B. (2001). The "untracking" of sedentary living: A call for action. *Pediatric Exercise Science, 13,* 347–356.

Corbin, C.B. (2002). Physical activity for everyone: What every physical educator should know about promoting lifelong physical activity. *Journal of Teaching Physical Education, 21,* 128–144.

Corbin, C., & Pangrazi, R. (1999). Physical activity for children: In pursuit of appropriate guidelines. *European Journal of Physical Education, 4,* 136–138.

Corbin, C., Pangrazi, R., & Le Masurier, G. (2004). Physical activity for children: Current patterns and guidelines. *Journal of Physical Activity and Health, 1,* 281.

Corbin, C., Pangrazi, R., & Welk, G. (1994). Toward an understanding of appropriate physical activity levels for youth. *Physical Activity and Fitness Research Digest, 1* (8), 1–8.

Couturier, L.E., Chepko, S., & Coughlin, M. (2005). Student voices—What middle and high school students have to say about physical education. *Physical Educator, 63* (4), 170–177.

Couturier, L.E., Chepko, S., & Coughlin, M. (2007). Whose gym is it? Gendered perspectives on middle and secondary school physical education. *Physical Educator, 64* (3), 152–157.

Darst, P., Pangrazi, R.P., Sariscsany, M., & Brusseau, P. (2011). *Dynamic physical education for secondary school students.* San Francisco: Benjamin Cummings.

Derry, J.A. (2002). Single-sex and coeducation physical education: Perspectives of adolescent girls and female physical education teachers. *Melpomene Journal, 21* (3), 21–27.

Dunton, G.F., Berrigan, D., Ballard-Barbash, R., Perna, F., Grauband, B.I., & Atienza, A.A. (2012). Differences in exercise intensity and duration of adolescents' sports and exercise across physical and social environments. *Research Quarterly for Exercise and Sport, 83* (3), 376–382.

Eather, N., Morgan, O.J., & Lubans, D.R. (2013). Improving the fitness and physical activity levels of primary school children: Results of the Fit-4-Fun group randomized controlled trial. *Preventive Medicine, 56,* 12–19.

Eime, R., Harvey, J., Sawyer, N., Craike, M., Symons, C., Polman, R., & Payne, W. (2013). Understanding contexts of adolescent female participation in sport and physical activity. *Research Quarterly for Exercise and Sport, 84,* 157–166.

Ennis, C.D. (2010). On their own: Preparing students for a lifetime. *Journal of Physical Education, Recreation and Dance, 81* (5), 17–22.

Ennis, C. (2011). Physical education curriculum priorities: Evidence for education and skillfulness. *Quest, 63,* 5–18.

Ericsson, K.A. (1996). The acquisition of expert performance: An introduction to some of the issues. In K.A. Ericsson (Ed.), *The road to excellence: The acquisition of expert performance in the arts and sciences, sports, and games* (pp. 1–50). Mahwah, NJ: Erlbaum.

Ericsson, K.A. (2001). The path to expert performance: Insights from the masters on how to improve performance by deliberate practice. In P. Thomas (Ed.), *Optimizing performance in golf* (pp. 1–57). Brisbane, Australia: Australian Academic Press.

Ericsson, K.A. (2002). Attaining excellence through deliberate practice: Insights from the study of expert performance. In M. Ferrari (Ed.), *The pursuit of excellence in education* (pp. 21–55). Hillsdale, NJ: Erlbaum.

Ericsson, K.A. (2003a). The search for general abilities and basic capacities: Theoretical implications from the modifiability and complexity of mechanisms mediating expert performance. In R.J. Sternberg & E.L. Grigorenko (Eds.), *Perspective on the psychology of abilities, competencies, and expertise* (pp. 93–125). Cambridge, UK: Cambridge University Press.

Ericsson, K.A. (2003b). The development of elite performance and deliberate practice: An update from the perspective of the expert-performance approach. In J. Strakes & K.A. Ericsson (Eds.), *Expert performance in sport: Recent advances in research on sport expertise* (pp. 49–81). Champaign, IL: Human Kinetics.

Ericsson, K.A. (2004). Deliberate practice and the acquisition and maintenance of expert performance in medicine and related domains. *Academic Medicine, 10,* S1–S12.

Ericsson K.A. (2006). The influence of experience and deliberate practice on the development of superior performance. In K.A. Ericsson, N. Chamess, P.J. Feltovich, & R.R. Hoffman (Eds.), *The Cambridge handbook of expertise and expert performance* (pp. 685–705). Cambridge, UK: Cambridge University Press.

Ericsson, K., Krampe, R., & Tesch-Romer, C. (1993). The role of deliberate practice in the acquisition of expert performance. *Psychological Review, 100* (3), 363–406.

Ericsson, K.A., & Lehman, A.C. (1996). Expert and exceptional performance: Evidence on maximal adaptations on task constraints. *Annual Review of Psychology, 47,* 273–305.

Espenschade, A.S., & Eckert, H.M. (1967). *Motor development.* Columbus, OH: Merrill.

Gallahue, D.L., Ozmun, J., & Goodway, J. (2012). *Understanding motor development: Infants, children, adolescents, adults.* New York: McGraw-Hill.

Gallahue, D.L., Ozmun, J., & Goodway, J. (2011). *Understanding motor development: Infants, children, adolescents, adults* (7th ed.). New York: McGraw-Hill.

Gao, Z., Lee, A., & Harrison, L. (2012). Understanding students' motivation in sport and physical education: From the Expectancy-Value Model and Self-Efficacy Theory perspectives. *Quest, 60,* 236–254.

Gao, Z., Lee, A.M., Ping, X., & Kosam, M. (2011). Effect of learning activity on students' motivation, physical activity levels and effort/persistence. *ICHPER-SD Journal of Research in Health, Physical Education, Recreation, Sport and Dance, 6* (1), 27–33.

Gao, Z., Lee, A.M., Solmon, M.A., & Zhang, T. (2009). Changes in middle school students' motivation toward physical education over one school year. *Journal of Teaching in Physical Education, 28,* 378–399.

Garn, A.C., Cothran, D.J., & Jenkins, J.M. (2011). A qualitative analysis of individual interest in middle school physical education: Perspective of early adolescents. *Physical Education and Sport Pedagogy, 16* (3), 223–236.

Garn, A.C., Ware, D.R., & Solmon, M.A. (2011). Student engagement in high school physical education: Do social motivation orientations matter? *Journal of Teaching in Physical Education, 30*, 84–98.

Gentile, A.M. (1972). A working model of skill acquisition with application to teaching. *Quest,* Monograph XVII, 3–23.

Graham, G., Holt/Hale, S., & Parker, M. (2013). *Children moving: A reflective approach to teaching physical education.* New York: McGraw-Hill.

Greenwood, M., Stillwell, J., & Byars, A. (2001). Activity preferences of middle school physical education students. *Physical Educator, 58* (1), 26–32.

Grieser, M., Vu, M.B., Bedimo-Rung, A.L., Neumark-Sztainer, D., Moody, J., Young, D.R., & Moe, S.G. (2006). Physical activities attitudes, preferences, and practices in African American, Hispanic, and Caucasian girls. *Health Education and Behavior, 33* (1), 40–51.

Griffin, L.L., & Butler, J.I. (2005). *Teaching games for understanding: Theory, research and practice.* Champaign, IL: Human Kinetics.

Griffin, L.L., Mitchell, S.A., & Oslin, J.L. (2006). *Teaching sport concepts and skills: A tactical games approach.* Champaign, IL: Human Kinetics.

Gruson, L.M. (1988). Rehearsal skill and musical competence: Does practice make perfect? In J.A. Sloboda (Ed.), *Generative processes in music* (pp. 91–112). Oxford, UK: Clarenden.

Haerens, L., Kirk, D., Cardon, G., De Bourdeauhuij, I., & Vansteenkiste, M. (2010). Motivation profiles for secondary school physical education and its relationship to the adoption of a physically active lifestyle among university students. *European Physical Education Review, 16* (2), 117–139.

Haibach, P.S., Reid, G., & Collier, D.J. (2011). *Motor learning and development.* Champaign, IL: Human Kinetics.

Hamilton, K., & White, K.M. (2008). Extending the theory of planned behavior: The role of self and social influences in predicting adolescent regular moderate-to-vigorous physical activity. *Journal of Sport and Exercise Science, 30*, 56–74.

Hannon, J.C., & Ratcliffe, T. (2005). Physical activity levels in coeducational and single-gender high school physical education settings. *Journal of Teaching in Physical Education, 24*, 149–164.

Haywood, K.M. (1986). *Life span motor development.* Champaign, IL: Human Kinetics.

Hewitt, J.E. (1965). Revision of the Dyer Backboard Tennis Test. *Research Quarterly, 36* (2), 153–157.

Hill, G., & Hannon, J.C. (2008). An analysis of middle school students' physical education physical activity preferences. *Physical Educator, 65* (4), 180–194.

Himberg, C., Hutchinson, G.E., & Roussell, J.M. (2003). *Teaching secondary physical education: Preparing adolescents to be active for life.* Champaign, IL: Human Kinetics.

Institute of Medicine of the National Academies. (2013). *Educating the student body: Taking physical activity and physical education to school.* Washington, DC: National Academy of Sciences. Available: www.iom.edu/studentbody.

InTime. (2001). *Content Standards.* Available: www.intime.uni.edu/model/content/cont.html.

Johnson, T.G., Prusak, K.A., Pennington, T., & Wilkinson, C. (2011). The effects of the type of skill test, choice, and gender on the situational motivation of physical education students. *Journal of Teaching in Physical Education, 30*, 281–295.

Kambas, A., Michalopoulou, M., Fatouros, I., Christoforidis, C., Manthou, E., Giannakidou, D., Venetsanou, F., Haberer, E., Chatzinikolaou, A., Gourgoulis, V., & Zimmer, R. (2012). The relationship between motor proficiency and pedometer-determined physical activity in young children. *Pediatric Exercise Science, 24*, 34–44.

Krampe, R.Th., & Ericsson, K.A. (1996). Maintaining excellence: Deliberate practice and elite performance in young and older pianists. *Journal of Experimental Psychology: General, 125*, 331–359.

Lloyd, M., Colley, R.C., & Tremblay, M.S. (2010). Advancing the debate on "fitness testing" for children: Perhaps we're riding the wrong animal. *Pediatric Exercise Science, 22*, 176–182.

Lounsbery, A., McKenzie, T., Trost, S., & Smith, N. (2011). Facilitators and barriers to adopting evidence-based physical education in elementary schools. *Journal of Physical Activity and Health, 8,* S17–S25.

Mandigo, J., Francis, N., Lodewyk, K., & Lopez, R. (2012). Physical literacy for educators. *Physical Education and Health Journal, 75* (3), 27–30.

Manitoba Education and Training, School Programs Division. (2000). *Physical education/health education: Manitoba curriculum framework of outcomes for active healthy lifestyles.* Available: www.edu.gov.mb.ca/k12/cur/physhlth/index.html.

Maxwell, J.P., Masters, R.S., Kerr, E., Weedon, E. (2001). The implicit benefit of learning without errors. *Quarterly Journal of Experimental Psychology 54*, 1049–1068.

McKenzie, T.L., Prochaska, J.J., Sallis, J.F., & LaMaster, K.J. (2004). Coeducational and single-sex physical education in middle schools: Impact on physical activity. *Research Quarterly for Exercise and Sport, 75* (4), 446–449.

McKenzie, T.L., Sallis, J.F., Prochaska, J.J., Conway, T.L., Marshall, S.J., & Rosengard, P. (2004). Evaluation of a two-year middle-school physical education intervention: M-SPAN. *Medicine and Science in Exercise and Sport, 36* (8), 1382–1388.

Mears, D. (2008). Curriculum diversity and young adult physical activity: Reflections from high school physical education. *Physical Educator, 65* (4), 195–207.

Mitchell, S., Oslin, J., & Griffin, L. (2006). *Teaching sport concepts and skills: A tactical games approach.* Champaign, IL: Human Kinetics.

Mohnsen, B. (2008). *Teaching middle school physical education: A standards-based approach for grades 5–8.* Champaign, IL: Human Kinetics.

Mohnsen, B. (Ed.). (2010). *Concepts and principles of physical education: What every student needs to know.* Reston, VA: NASPE.

Mosston, M., & Ashworth, S. (2002). *Teaching physical education* (Grade 5 ed.). San Francisco: Benjamin Cummings.

NASPE. (1992). *Outcomes of quality physical education programs.* Reston, VA: Author.

NASPE. (1995). *Moving into the future: National standards for physical education.* Reston, VA: Author.

NASPE. (2004). *Moving into the future: National standards for physical education* (2nd ed.). Reston, VA: Author.

NASPE. (2008). *Comprehensive school physical activity programs* [Position statement]. Reston, VA: Author.

NASPE. (2009a). *Appropriate instructional practice guidelines for high school physical education.* Reston, VA: Author.

NASPE. (2009b). *Appropriate instructional practice guidelines for middle school physical education.* Reston, VA: Author.

NASPE. (2009c). *Appropriate instructional practice guidelines for elementary school physical education.* Reston, VA: Author.

NASPE. (2009d). *Appropriate use of instructional technology in physical education* [Position statement]. Reston, VA: National Association for Sport and Physical Education.

NASPE. (2010). *PE metrics: Assessing national standards 1–6 in elementary school.* Reston, VA: Author.

NASPE. (2011). *PE metrics: Assessing national standards 1–6 in secondary school.* Reston, VA: Author.

NASPE. (2012). *Instructional framework for fitness education in physical education.* Reston, VA: Author.

National Academy of Sciences. (1996). *National science education standards.* Washington, DC: National Academy Press.

National Council of Teachers of Mathematics. (2006). *Curriculum focal points for prekindergarten through grade 8 mathematics: A quest for coherence.* Reston, VA: Author.Ntoumanis, N., Pensgaard, A., Martin, C., & Pipe, K. (2004). An idiographic analysis of amotivation in compulsory school physical education. *Journal of Sport and Exercise Science, 26,* 197–214.

Ntoumanis, N., Pensgaard, A., Martin, C., & Pipe, K. (2004). An idiographic analysis of amotivation in compulsory school physical education. *Journal of Sport & Exercise Science, 26,* 197–214.

Office of Student Learning and Professional Development. (2010). *Prince William County Public Schools physical education curriculum guide grades k–12.* Available: http://hpe-curriculum-resources.pwcs.healthpe.schoolfusion.us/modules/locker/files/get_group_file.phtml?fid=9154582&gid=1450982.

Ohio State Board of Education. (2009). *Physical education standards.* Available: http://education.ohio.gov/GD/Templates/Pages/ODE/ODEDetail.aspx?Page=3&TopicRelationID=1793&Content=132142.

Ommundsen, Y. (2006). Pupils' self-regulation in physical education: The role of motivational climates and differential achievement goals. *European Physical Education Review, 12* (3), 289–315.

O'Neill, J.R., Pate, R.R., & Liese, A.D. (2011). Descriptive epidemiology of dance participation in adolescents. *Research Quarterly for Exercise and Sport, 82* (3), 373–380.

Pangrazi, R.P. (2010). Chasing unachievable outcomes. *Quest, 62,* 323–333.

Pangrazi, R.P., & Beighle, A. (2010). *Dynamic physical education for elementary school children.* San Francisco: Benjamin Cummings.

Pangrazi, R.P., Corbin, C.B., & Welk, G.J. (1996). Physical activity for children and youth. *Journal of Health, Physical Education, Recreation and Dance, 67*(4), 38–43.

Patnode, C.D., Lytle, L.A., Erickson, D.J., Sirard, J.R., Barr-Anderson, D.J., & Story, M. (2011). Physical activity and sedentary activity patterns among children and adolescents: A latent class analysis approach. *Journal of Physical Activity and Health, 8,* 457–467.

Penney, D., Brooker, R., Hay, P., & Gillespie, L. (2009). Curriculum, pedagogy and assessment: Three message systems of schooling and dimensions of quality physical education. *Sport, Education and Society, 14* (4), 421–442.

Penney, D., & Chandler, T. (2000). Physical education: What future(s)? *Sport, Education and Society, 5* (1), 71–87.

Physical Activity Guidelines for Americans. Available: www.health.gov/paguidelines.

Placek, J.H. (1983). Conceptions of success in teaching: Busy, happy, and good? In T. Templin & J. Olsen (Eds.), *Teaching in physical education* (pp. 46–56). Champaign, IL: Human Kinetics.

Portman, P. (2003). Are physical education classes encouraging students to be physically active?: Experiences of ninth grades in their last semester of required physical education. *Physical Educator, 63* (3), 150–161.

Prochaska, J.J., Sallis, J.F., Slymen, D.J., & McKenzie, T.L. (2003). A longitudinal study of children's enjoyment of physical education. *Pediatric Exercise Science, 15,* 170–178.

Prusak, K. A., & Darst, P.W. (2002). Effects of types of walking activities on actual choices by adolescent female physical education students. *Journal of Teaching in Physical Education, 21,* 230–241.

Prusak, K.A., Treasure, D.C., Darst, P.W., & Pangrazi, R. (2004). The effects of choice on the motivation of adolescent girls in physical education. *Journal of Teaching in Physical Education, 23,* 19–29.

Qualifications and Curriculum Authority. (2007). *Physical education: The national curriculum for England.* Available: www.qca.org.uk/curriculum.

Qualifications, Curriculum and Assessment Authority. (2000). *Physical education in the national curriculum in Wales.* Cardiff, Wales: ACCAC.

Rarick, G.L. (1961). *Motor development during infancy and childhood.* Madison, WI: College.

Rink, J. (2009). *Designing the physical education curriculum: Promoting active lifestyles.* Boston: McGraw-Hill Higher Education.

Rovegno, I., & Bandauer, D. (2013). *Elementary physical education: Curriculum and instruction.* Burlington, MA: Jones & Bartlett Publishing.

Ruiz, L.M., Graupera, J.L., Moreno, J.A., & Rico, I. (2010). Social preferences for learning among adolescents. *Journal of Teaching in Physical Education, 29*, 3–20.

Sallis, J.F., McKenzie, T.L., Beets, M.W., Beighle, A., Erwin, H., & Lee, S. (2012). Physical education's role in public health: Steps forward and backward over 20 years and HOPE for the future. *Research Quarterly for Exercise and Sport, 83,* (2), 125–135.

Schmidt, R.A., & Bjork, R.A. (1992). New conceptualizations of practice: Common principles in three paradigms suggest new concepts for training. *Psychological Science, 3*, 207–217.

Schmidt, R.A., & Wrisberg, C.A. (2008). *Motor learning and performance: A situation-based learning approach* (Grade 4 ed.). Champaign, IL: Human Kinetics.

Schuldheisz, J.M., & van der Mars, H. (2001). Active supervision and students' physical activity in middle school physical education. *Journal of Teaching in Physical Education, 21*, 75–90.

Schulz, R., & Curnow, C. (1988). Peak performance and age among superathletes: Track and field, swimming, baseball, tennis, and golf. *Journal of Gerontology: Psychological Sciences, 43*, 113–120.

Seidentop, D. (2002). Content knowledge in physical education. *Journal of Teaching in Physical Education, 21*, 368–377.

Seidentop, D., & van der Mars, H. (2012). *Introduction to physical education, fitness and sport.* New York: McGraw-Hill.

Senne, T.A., & Lund, J.L. (2012). *Navigating the program evaluation process for PETE & kinesiology: A roadmap for success.* Reston, VA: NASPE.

Shea, J.B., & Morgan, R.L. (1979). Contextual interference effects on the acquisition, retention, and transfer of a motor skill. *Journal of Experimental Psychology: Human Learning and Memory, 5*, 179–187.

Shen, B., Wingert, R.K., Weidong, L., Haichun, S., & Rukavina, P.B. (2010). An amotivational model in physical education. *Journal of Teaching in Physical Education, 29*, 72–84.

Silverman, S., Tyson, L.A., & Morford, L.M. (1988). Relationships of organization, time, and student achievement in physical education. *Teaching and Teacher Education, 4*, 247–257.

Simon, H.A., & Chase, W.G. (1973). Skill in chess. *American Scientist, 61*, 394–403.

Simpson, E.J. (1972). The classification of educational objectives in the psychomotor domain. Washington, D.C.: Gryphon House. Available: www.nwlink.com/~donclark/hrd/bloom.html.

Sloboda, J.A., Davidson, J.W., Howe, M.J.A., & Moore, D.G. (1996). The role of practice in the development of performing musicians. *British Journal of Psychology, 87*, 287–309.

Smith, M.A., & St. Pierre, P. (2009). Secondary students' perceptions of enjoyment in physical education: An American and English perspective. *The Physical Educator, 66* (4), 209–221.

Solmon, M., & Lee, A.M. (1996). Entry characteristics, practice variables, and cognition: Student mediation of instruction. *Journal of Teaching in Physical Education, 15*, 136–150.

Spessato, B., Gabbard, C., & Valentini, N. (2013). The role of motor competence and body mass index in children's physical activity levels in physical education classes. *Journal of Teaching in Physical Education, 32*, 118–130.

Standage, M., Duda, J., & Ntoumanis, N. (2003). Predicting motivational regulations in physical education: The interplay between dispositional goal orientations, motivational climate and perceived competence. *Journal of Sport Sciences, 21*, 631–647.

State of New Jersey Department of Education. (2009). *New Jersey core curriculum content standards—Comprehensive health and physical education.* Available: www.nj.gov/education/cccs/standards/2/.

Stodden, D.F., Goodway, J.L., Langendorfer, S.J., Roberton, M., Rudisill, M.E., Garcia, C., & Garcia, L.E. (2008). A developmental perspective on the role of motor skill competence in physical activity: An emergent relationship. *Quest, 60*, 290–306.

Stodden, D., Langendorfer, S., & Roberton, M. (2009). The association between motor skill competence and physical fitness in young adults. *Research Quarterly for Exercise and Sport, 80* (2), 223–229.

Strakes, J.L., Deakin, J., Allard, F., Hodges, N.J., & Hayes, A. (1996). Deliberate practice in sports: What is it anyway? In K.A. Ericsson (Ed.), *The road to excellence: The acquisition of expert performance in the arts and sciences, sports, and games* (pp. 81–106). Mahwah, NJ: Erlbaum.

Strong, W.B., Malina, R.M., Blimkie, C.J., Daniels, S.R., Dishman, R.K., Gutin, B., Hergenroeder, A.C., Must, A., Nixon, P., Pivarnik, J.M., Rowland, T., Trost, S., & Trudeau, F. (2005). Evidence based physical activity for school-age youth. *Journal of Pediatrics, 146*, 732–737.

Stuart, J.H., Biddle, S.H., O'Donovan, T.M., & Nevill, M.E. (2005). Correlates of participation in physical activity for adolescent girls: A systematic review of recent literature. *Journal of Physical Activity and Health, 2*, 423–434.

Subramaniam, P.R. (2009). Motivational effects of interest on student engagement and learning in physical education. *International Journal of Physical Education, 46* (2), 11–19.

Superintendent of Public Instruction, Washington. (2008). *Washington State k–12 health and fitness learning standards.* Olympia, WA: Author.

Treanor, L., Graber, K., Housner, L., & Weigand, R. (1998). Middle school students' perceptions of coeducational and same-sex physical education classes. *Journal of Teaching in Physical Education, 18*, 43–56.

Treasure, D.C., & Roberts, G.C. (2001). Students' perceptions of the motivational climate, achievement beliefs, and satisfaction in physical education. *Research Quarterly for Exercise and Sport, 72* (2), 165–175.

Trost, S.G., Pate, R.R., Saunders, R., Ward, D.S., Dowda, M., & Felton, G. (1997). A prospective study of the determinants of physical activity in rural fifth-grade children. *Preventive Medicine, 26*, 257–263.

U.S. Department of Health and Human Services. (2008). *Physical activity guidelines for Americans*. Washington, D.C.: Author. Available at www.health.gov/paguidelines.

Van Beurden, E., Barnett, L.M., Zask, A., Dietrich, U.C., Brooks, L.O., & Beard, J. (2003). Can we skill and activate children through primary school physical education lessons? "Move it groove it"—A collaborative health promotion intervention. *Preventive Medicine, 36*, 493–501.

van der Mars, H. (2006). Time and learning in physical education. In D. Kirk, D. MacDonald, & M. O'Sullivan (Eds.), *The handbook of physical education* (pp. 191–213). London: Sage.

Wang, J., Castelli, D.M., Liu, W., Bian, W., & Tan, J. (2010). Re-conceptualizing physical education programs from an ecological perspective. *Asian Journal of Exercise and Sports Science, 7* (1), 43–53.

Ward, J., Wilkinson, C., Graser, S.V., & Prusak, K.A. (2008). Effects of choice on student motivation and physical activity behavior in physical education. *Journal of Teaching in Physical Education, 27*, 385–398.

Whitehead, M. (2001). The concept of physical literacy. *European Journal of Physical Education, 6*, 127–138.

Wichita Public Schools. (2009). *Grade-level and program standards*. Available: http://learningservices.usd259.org/modules/locker/files/group_files.phtml?parent=7 379728&gid=1543081&sessionid=58b5d83fef47ccfa8 c19e2616913619f.

Wickstrom, R.L. (1970). *Fundamental motor patterns*. Philadelphia: Lea & Febiger.

Wilkinson, C., & Bretzing, R. (2011). High school girls' perceptions of selected physical activities. *The Physical Educator, 68* (2), 58–65.

Xiang, P., McBride, R., & Guan, J. (2004). Children's motivation in elementary school physical education: A longitudinal study. *Research Quarterly for Exercise and Sport, 75* (1), 71–80.

Xu, F., & Liu, W. (2013). A review of middle school students' attitudes toward physical activity. In L.E. Ciccomascolo & E.C. Sullivan (Eds.), *The dimensions of physical education* (pp. 286–295). Burlington, MA: Jones & Bartlett Learning.

Yli-Piipari, S., Leskinen, E., Jaakkola, T., & Liukkonen, J. (2012). Predictive role of physical education motivation: The developmental trajectories of physical activity during grades 7–9. *Research Quarterly for Exercise and Sport, 83* (4), 560–569.

Zhang, T., Solmon, M., Kosma, M., Carson, R.L., & Gu, X. (2011). Need support, need satisfaction, intrinsic motivation, and physical activity participation among middle school students. *Journal of Teaching in Physical Education, 30*, 51–68.

About the Authors

About SHAPE America

The Society of Health and Physical Educators (SHAPE America)—formerly the American Alliance for Health, Physical Education, Recreation and Dance (AAHPERD)—is the nation's largest organization of professionals involved in physical education, physical activity, dance, school health and sport: all specialties related to achieving an active, healthy lifestyle. SHAPE America's mission is to advance professional practice and promote research related to health and physical education, physical activity, dance and sport.

About the Principal Writers

Lynn Couturier, DPE, is the chair of the physical education department at State University of New York at Cortland and a former president of the National Association for Sport and Physical Education (NASPE). She has made significant contributions to physical education for more than 25 years. She chaired AAHPERD's Curriculum Framework Task Force, which revised the National Standards for K-12 Physical Education and developed new grade-level outcomes, which are contained in this book. Dr. Couturier also served as a member of NASPE's task force for revising the National Standards for Initial Physical Education Teacher Education and has served in numerous capacities  for NASPE, AAHPERD, the National Council for Accreditation of Coaching Education and the Eastern District Association of AAHPERD. She has published in the areas of physical education pedagogy, coaching education and women's sport history. Dr. Couturier earned her BS degree in physical education from Springfield College in 1981, an MS degree in biomechanics from the University of Illinois at Urbana–Champaign in 1985, and a doctorate of physical education from Springfield College in 1986. Her postdoctoral study includes earning a graduate certificate in advanced feminist studies from the University of Massachusetts–Amherst in 2002 and a master's degree in American studies from Trinity College in 2007.

Stevie Chepko, EdD, is vice president for program review for the Council for the Accreditation of Educator Preparation. She is a well-respected authority on performance-based standards, teaching for mastery and assessment in physical education. A hallmark of Dr. Chepko's professional service has been the development of materials that engage practitioners and reflect best practices in the field. She served as chair of the task force named to revise the National Standards for Initial Physical Education Teacher Education and served on the AAHPERD Curriculum Framework Task Force that developed the National Standards & Grade-Level Outcomes for K-12 Physical Education. Dr. Chepko's commit-

ment to the profession has been recognized with many honors, including the AAHPERD Honor Award; Eastern District Association (EDA) Vermont, Massachusetts and South Carolina Honor Awards; NASPE's Joy of Effort Award; selection as an inaugural fellow in the North American Society of Health, Physical Education, Recreation, Sport and Dance; and EDA Memorial Lecturer. She is a member of the West Virginia University Physical Education Hall of Fame and the Castleton College Athletic Hall of Fame. Dr. Chepko earned her undergraduate degree from West Virginia University, attended the University of North Carolina at Greensboro for further graduate work, and completed her EdD in curriculum and instruction and sport history at Temple University.

Shirley Holt/Hale, PhD, is a retired physical educator from Linden Elementary School in Oak Ridge, Tennessee, where she taught physical education for 38 years. Dr. Holt/Hale has served as president of both AAHPERD and the National Association for Sport and Physical Education and is a former National Elementary Physical Education Teacher of the Year. She brought to the writing team strong beliefs in student learning and skill acquisition; a balanced curriculum of educational gymnastics, dance and rhythms; and the foundational skills of games and sports. She is the coauthor of *Children Moving: A Reflective Approach to Teaching Physical Education* (9th edition), author of *On the Move: Lesson Plans to Accompany Children Moving*, and contributing author for three other texts. Dr. Holt/Hale serves as a consultant in elementary physical education curriculum and assessment throughout the United States.

SHAPE America Membership
Become the Best Teacher You Can Be

SHAPE America – Society of Health and Physical Educators (formerly AAHPERD) delivers all the best professional development and resources for school-based health educators and physical education, recreation, dance or sport professionals.

- Members select one or more of the idea-packed, peer-reviewed journals designed for all areas of concentration.
  - ✓ *Journal of Physical Education, Recreation & Dance*
  - ✓ *Research Quarterly for Exercise and Sport*
  - ✓ *American Journal of Health Education*
  - ✓ *Strategies: A Journal for Physical and Sport Educators*

- SHAPE America National and District Conventions are the world's largest gathering of health, physical education, recreation, dance and sport professionals – an unparalleled professional development opportunity.

- SHAPE America offers more than 200 titles for you to choose from. Stock your library with the newest releases, best sellers and resources that you can use to help move your school or business forward.

- Accessible, informative and affordable! SHAPE America's free publications will help you build your educational portfolio and keep you up-to-date on issues, events, teaching resources and special offers.
  - ✓ *Momentum*, our quarterly newsletter
  - ✓ *Et Cetera*, our weekly e-newsletter
  - ✓ *Quest**
  - ✓ *Measurement in Physical Education and Exercise Science**
  - ✓ *Journal of Sports Sciences**
    * log into your online account to view

- The SHAPE America Professional Development Center offers year-round learning opportunities, including workshops, distance learning, conferences and webinars for health and physical educators. Visit www.shapeamerica.org/profdev for an up-to-date listing of what's available.

- Launching in Fall 2014: Our brand new online community where members can connect with each other, drive collaboration, ignite conversation and create an industry knowledge base that is accessible anytime.

- Members save with discounts on insurance, professional development resources, books and other products, as well as conference and convention registrations.

SHAPE America — SOCIETY OF HEALTH AND PHYSICAL EDUCATORS

health. moves. minds.